Georgia Sharpshooter

Georgia Sharpshooter

The Civil War Diary and Letters of
William Rhadamanthus Montgomery
1839–1906

George F. Montgomery, Jr.
Editor

Mercer Univeristy Press
Macon, Georgia
1997

Georgia Sharpshooter
The Civil War Diary and Letters
of William Rhadamanthus Montgomery
Edited by George F. Montgomery, Jr.

© 1997
All rights reserved.
Mercer University Press
6316 Peake Road
Macon, Georgia 31210-3960

Library of Congress Cataloging-in-Publication Data

Montgomery, William Rhadamanthus, 1839–1906
Georgia Sharpshooter: The Civil War Diary and Letters of William
Rhadamanthus Montgomery, 1839–1906 /
George F. Montgomery Jr., editor.
pp.
Includes Bibliographical References (p.) and index.
ISBN 0-86554-572-3
1. Montgomery, William Rhadamanthus, 1839-1906 — Diaries.
2. Montgomery, William Rhadamanthus, 1839-1906 —
Correspondence. 3. Confederate States of America. Army. South
Carolina Infantry Regiment, 2nd. 4. Soldiers — Georgia — Marietta —
Diaries. 5. Shooters of Firearms — Georgia — Marietta — Diaries.
6. Soldiers — Georgia — Marietta — Correspondence. 7. Shooters of
Firearms — Civil War, 1861 — 1865 — Personal narratives, Confederate.
9. Marietta (Ga.) — Biography. I. Montgomery, Jr., George, (George F.),
1915 — .
II. Title.
E577.5.M66
973.7'4757 — dc21   97–21316
                                                         CIP

Table of Contents

Photographs after page 58

Preface

Sometime after 1891, an auditor from Washington, D.C. traveled to Marietta, Georgia, in Cobb County. The auditor visited the courthouse and asked to see the county clerk, a war veteran named William Rhadamanthus Montgomery. The auditor received full compliance from Mr. Montgomery and had much success in confirming the records in the courthouse.

The only problem, however, was that the auditor could find no records prior to the war. He told the clerk that all the records were 100 percent in order, except that he could find no records prior to 1865, and could the clerk explain this. Montgomery, with firm consternation, replied that "Yes, there is an explanation." Montgomery continued, "that was the date that General Sherman, the son-of-a-bitch, came through Marietta burning our homes, city buildings, and records, and confiscating our food and stock. He is now dead and in hell and I'm glad of it." The auditor asked if that could be put in writing, and so it was.

William Rhadamanthus Montgomery was born 15 February 1839 at Standing Peachtree, in DeKalb County, Georgia. He died 30 November 1906 at his home on the corner of Cherokee and Montgomery Streets in Marietta, Georgia. He was married twice, first to Emma Jane Northcutt (5 January 1847−21 July 1894), and second to Anna Towers (26 August 1855−3 May 1906).

Early in 1861, Montgomery joined the Palmetto Guards Second South Carolina Volunteers Bonhams Brigade. His first combat action was at Fairfax Courthouse on 17 July 1861. This was followed by the battles of First Bull Run and Manassas. Montgomery was present at some of the most memorable battles of the Civil War. Among them were Chickahominy, Seven Pines, Malvern Hill, Manassas, Sharpsburg, Fredricksburg, Gettysburg, Chickamauga, Lookout Mountain, the Wilderness, Spottsylvania, and Cold Harbor.

In a letter to his mother and sister dated 7 May 1863, he said "We are in camp to ourselves & are known as the 1st Geo 'sharpshooters' but have no commissions yet." Montgomery received his letter of commission from James A. Seddon, secretary of war, C. S. A., dated 17 June 1863, appointing him "First Lieutenant, Third Georgia Battalion, Sharpshooters."

Wounded seven or eight times, Montgomery remained in service throughout the entire war. After Lee surrendered, Montgomery learned of a regiment that was still fighting in South Carolina. He walked the entire distance from Marietta only to find out when he arrived that regiment had also just surrendered.

Montgomery survived the war and returned to Marietta where he lived out the rest of his days. Years after the war, Montgomery returned to visit Fredricksburg and met a number of former Union soldiers from New Jersey. The meeting was one of honor and respect, and very friendly — a witness to the civility and integrity of all present. The subject arose, however, of a sword that Montgomery had acquired at Gettysburg, and it so happened that the sword belonged to a member of the ranks of the soldiers from New Jersey. The last four letters in the present collection discuss this event. Presented here, they reveal a respect for both sides that is often unheard of.

The diary and the letters contained herein is a testament to his time as a soldier during the Civil War. But as the diary and letters indicate, the war was not the end all of his life. His love for his first wife and his family far surpassed any national conflict that could have arisen. His loyalty for the South was surpassed only by his loyalty for and to his family.

Thanks goes to Mrs. Cora Fletcher, secretary of Westminster by the Sea Presbyterian Church who spent countless hours in typing the manuscript.

This book is dedicated to James T. Anderson, Jr. and Emma Katharine Anderson (brother and sister), the grandson and granddaughter of William Rhadamanthus Montgomery. Because of their interest in the Montgomery family, this diary has been preserved.

The Diary of
William Rhadamanthus
Montgomery

William Rhadamanthus Montgomery
1839 – 1906
[Chronology]

Born: February 15, 1839, at Standing Peachtree, DeKalb County (now Fulton County), Georgia.

Died: November 30, 1906, at his home on the corner of Cherokee and Montgomery Streets, Marietta, Georgia.

Married: (1) May 17, 1866, to Emma Jane Northcutt (January 5, 1847 – July 21,1894)
(2) September 12, 1895, to Anna Towers (August 26, 1855 – May 3, 1906)

Parents: James Floyd Montgomery of Standing Peachtree, Georgia. (September 10, 1813 – June 8, 1847), Elizabeth Ann Young (August 1, 1816 – November 10, 1890). Married January 12, 1837, in Cobb County, Georgia.

Paternal Grandparents: Major James McComb Montgomery of Standing Peachtree, Georgia. (May 19, 1770 – October 6, 1842), Nancy Farlow (October 7, 1781 – July 27, 1842) Married November 14, 1797, in Hancock County, Georgia.

Maternal Grandparents: Samuel Young of Cobb County, Georgia (December 272, 1783 – January 26, 1856), Margaret Wilson Long (January 3, 1791 – December 16, 1856). Married March 8, 1807, in Abbeville District, South Carolina.

The following is copied from War Notes of W. R. Montgomery, written by him in a tablet, now in the possession of Mrs. Annie Montgomery DuPre, Marietta, GA. Copied by EKA November 1960.

Battles in which I fought:

Skirmish near Fairfax Court House, July 17, 1861.

Skirmish at German Town, same day.

1. Bat. on Bull Run, Thursday July 18/61
2. 1st Bat. Manassas, Sunday July 21/61
3. Bat. Drainsville, Dec. 20th/61 on a foraging party, skirmishing daily for two or three weeks, at Dam #1 & 2 near York Town. Lost many men.
4. May 4/62, Skirmish at Williamsburg Sunday evening.
5. May 5/62, Battle, Williamsburg all day in the rain, whipped the fight but loss heavy. Several skirmishes on the Chickahominy.
6. Bat. Seven Pines — hard one — 7 days around Richmond.
7. Cold Harbor — hard one.
8. Gain's Mill — " "
9. Gain's Ford
10. Savage Station, Sunday — Hard one.
11. Frasers Farm, Monday — Hard one.
12. Malvern Hill, Tuesday — Hard one.
13. Cedar Mt., near Culpepper C.H. — Hard one
     Thorough Gap — hard skirmish
14. 2nd Bat. Manassas — a hard one, though we routed them.
15. Boonsboro, Md. Had to fall back.
16. Md. Heights — in the Capture of Harpers Ferry.
17. Sharpsburg — a big one.
     Skirmish at Shepards Town.
18. Fredricksburg, 13th Dec. 1862 — a hard one in the snow.

19. May 3/63, Chancellorsville—a big one—3 days. Jackson killed. Our loss heavy.
20. Salem Church—a hard one—May/63.
21. Gettysburg, 3 days
22. Chicamauga, Tenn.—Sunday, with Longstreet when he broke the lines.
23. Several hot skirmishes around Lookout Mt. & Chattanooga.
24. Louden, Tenn.
25. Lanoah's Station.
26. Campbell Station near Knoxville. Several hot skirmishes near Knoxville—Hot fight on Picket.
27. Charge at Knoxville Ft. Sanders.
28. Skirmish at Bean Station near Tate Springs, Tenn.
29. Wilderness, VA 6th May/64.
30. Spottsylvania—or Horsehoe—one of the hardest of the war.
31. Cold Harbor—June 3/64. A big one. I was wounded. A good many skirmishes below Richmond, at Deep Bottom & on the James River.
32. Charge at the Crator, Petersburg.
33. Battles & skirmishes near Petersburg.
Hard skirmishing form then on until the surrender.

W. D. Anderson & myself left Marietta,—1861, for Charleston, then the seat of war. I joined the Palmetto Guards 2nd South Carolina Vol's Bonhams Brigade. The 1st Regt S.C.V. was commanded by Col. Maxey Gregg who was afterwards made Brig Genl. & was killed at Fredricksburg. The 2d (my Regt) was commanded by Col. J. B. Kershaw, afterwards made Maj. Genl. This then composed at that time Bonham's Brigade. We were ordered to Richmond on or about— 1861. These two Regts were the first troops that landed in Richmond. After some ten days, we were ordered to Manasssas Junction & went into camp on Bull Run. Were the first at Manassas or Bull Run. In two or three weeks, was ordered to Fairfax C.H. (only our two Regts), in about fifteen miles of Washington.

On Wednesday, July 17, 1861, the Grand Army of U. S. under command of Genl McDowell came on us. I was on picket two miles from Fairfax at Aquitlinc Creek. We skirmished with their van guard back to Fairfax where we expected to make a stand, but when we got there I found our army by orders was retreating or falling back on Bull run. Our Company, the Palmetto Guards, brought up the rear in good stile to Countervail where we were relieved. The 3d Regt S.C.V. under Col. Bacon & the 7th Regt S.C.V. under Col. Cash was joined to our Brigade.

On the 18th July 1861, the Yankies attacked our front at Mitchel's Ford. We were ordered out to meet them & made them "git". They moved down the River and attacked there Brig Genl Longstreet, who made the fur fly. This was Thursday. All was then quiet except picket fighting until Sunday morning July 21, when Genl McDowell threw his whole force on our left at Stone Bridge. The Yankies were pushing our men back, having ten to one. Two of our Regts 2d & 3rd were ordered to the Battlefield. We got there none too soon. As soon as we could get properly in line, they showed us the Yanks and we went for them with that old rebel yell. We drove them, & after the second charge they gave way, & the general stampede & rout commenced. The Palmetto Guards (my Co.) was deployed as skirmishers & followed them to Cubb Run, 3 miles, & captured everything they had left. It was a grand rout.

On Tuesday, the 23d, we were ordered to Vienna & thence to Fall's Church & thence Munsons (?) & Masons Hill in sight of Washington City. We remained there until some time in the fall & then fell back to Countervail & Bull Run & went into Winter Quarters for the winter.

On Dec. 20/61, we went out on a foraging party to get forage for the horses. Met the Yankies on similar mission at a little town called Drainsville. Got our wagons loaded and to the rear and had a hot fight for about two or three hours. Our loss about two hundred. Both sides drew off & we went back to camp.

About Mch 8th/62, we fell back to the Rappahanoc, and soon after to Richmond, and from there sent by boat to Yorktown, where we fought daily for several weeks, skirmishing at Dam #1 & #2, and across Kiff & Warwic Creek.

On May 4th, our whole army commenced the retreat up the Peninsula toward Richmond. My Co.

was detailed with four Ala. Cos under Maj Gracy, afterward Genl & killed at P—, to bring up the rear of the Army. We commenced the retreat Saturday night and arrived at Williamsburg Sunday morning without hindrance, but on Sunday evening we had a nice little skirmish. Longstreet was ordered back & we fought all day Monday the 5th in the rain. We won the battle, but on Tuesday began our retreat again.

On Wednesday, near West Point, we had a nice little fight, drove the Yanks back & captured 74 prisoners. We crossed the Chicohominie at or near New Kent Court House & took position up the River in six miles of Richmond with our own command completely worn out. Stonewall Jackson & his Army was in the valley & we got good news from him. May 30th, we fought the battle of Seven Pines. Our loss was heavy, but we whiped the fight. Genl Johnston was wounded & Genl Lee took command of the Army.

On the 26th of June, the 7 days of Battles around Richmond commenced at Ashland, sixteen miles from Richmond. I was in the Battles: Mechanicsville, Cold Harbor, Gain's Mill, Savage Station, Fraser's Farm, & Malvern Hill. When the battles ended we had driven the Yankies near forty miles under cover of their gun boats at Harrisons Landing. Our loss was about 16,000, the enemy something more.

On the 9th of August, 1862, we fought the Battle near Culpepper C.H., called Cedar Run & Slaughter Mt. We whipped them.

Genl Stonewall advanced, got in the rear of the Yankies, captured Manassas with all its stores & fell back some eight miles to the old Battlefield of Manassas. Genl Longstreet, our Corps, followed, cut our way through Thorough Gap Aug. 29/62, & joined old Stonewall none too soon. On the 30th of Aug., the big battle of Manassas commenced & it was bloody. We routed them but our loss was heavy.

On Sept. 7th, we had waded the Potomac at Leesburg & was camped at Fredrick, Md., about worn out. From thence we marched to Hagerstown & then returned to Boonsborough & had a hard battle & got rather worsted but not routed. McLaw's Div. (mine) was ordered to Maryland Heights overlooking Harper's Ferry. Had a hard battle. Harper's Ferry surrendered to us 13,000 men, 76 cannon & everything they had. We then were ordered at quick time to Sharpsburg—got there none too soon. We held them with their 150,000 with 35,000 for three days—drove them at every point. Our loss was about 8,000. After three days hard fighting at Sharpsburg, we waded the Potomac near Sheppardstown in Va. All of us bout gone up. This was in Sept. 1862.

We rested up for a while & then were ordered to Fredricksburg. Met the new commander, Genl Burnsides, and on the 13th Dec/62, we had the big Battle of Fredricksburg. We whiped them badly, though our loss was heavy but not near so great as theirs. I was in front of Mareys Heights. My Col. (Tom Cook) was killed, also my Genl. T.R.R.Cobb was killed. It was a hot time in the old town.

We then went back near the town into winter quarters, and then had a quiet time until May 25/63. Then came on the big battle of Chancellorsville in which the odds against us was 80,000. We licked them, though our loss was heavy. Stonewall Jackson and many privates & genl officers were killed.

Salem Church or Brick Church—Sunday morning the whole line in our front surrendered after a hard, hard battle Saturday until 9 o'clock in the night, and after hard fighting Sunday morning. Our command was then ordered back quick time in the direction of Fredricksburg to meet Genl Sedgwick who had crossed the river and was coming up in our rear with 22,000 men. Met him Sunday, and had a good battle & halted them for the night. On the next day (morning) we closed in on them in good stile and drove them across the river—47,000 to 127,000. We then went back to camp near Fredricksburg.

On June 3d, we commenced our march to Gettysburg, wading the Potomac at Williamsport, Md. We then advanced into Penn., almost in sight of Harrisburg, then back and met the Yankies at Gettysburg. I was in the two grand charges made by Longstreet and continually skirmishing for 3 or 4 days. We held the battlefield for two days & then retired to the Potomac. Had a hard battle near Funkstown in which I lost several men. We then crossed the Potomac at Falling Waters, again in old Va.

In Sept/63, we were sent to Ga. Got to Ringgold Saturday night before the big battle on Sunday. Was in the grand charge there when Longstreets Corps broke the lines. Our loss was estimated at 8,000. We then went near Chattanooga, and had quite a number of skirmishes in which we lost many good men. Our command was then ordered to Knoxville. When we got to Louden, Tenn., we crossed the Tenn. River on a pontoon. Had a fight at Lanoor's Station and also a hard fight at Campbell's Station near Knoxville on the 16th Nov.

We had a great deal of hard skirmishing around Knoxville. On the morning of Nov. 29th/63, we assaulted the Fort. We got on top & in the Fort but could not hold it & had to fall back after losing about 800 men in thirty minutes. Afterwards, we fell back to Rogersville, near Tate Springs, Tenn. It was bitter cold. The whole earth covered with snow. Half our men barefooted & almost destitute of clothing & nothing to eat. When we got to Rogersville, we drew our ear of corn to the man as rations & no fodder as one of the boys said. We had a skirmish in which I took at the Cross Roads known as Bean Station, in which we captured forty—odd wagons loaded with provisions. The first wagon I got in was loaded with brown sugar & roasted coffee in the grain. I was not long in filling my haversack.

We then crossed the Holston River and went into quarters for the winter near Morristown. We remained there until I do not remember when, until some time in the spring. Then marched on to Greenville, Bulls Gap, & from there Bristol, VA. & from there Lynchburg & then on to Charlottsville & from there to Gordonsville, having almost made a circuit of the Confederacy. We arrived at Gordonsville in, I think, the latter part of April. Got orders on the 5th of May to march in the direction of the wilderness.

We halted about midnight to rest. About 2 o'clock May 6th, we got orders to move at once as Genl Grant was pressing our forces. We were 8 miles from the battlefield. We quicked & double quicked 8 miles & met the Yankies at Parker's Store on Plank Road. Our men were falling back fast—almost routed. We took the right of the road & Gordon the left. We made music for about two & drove the whole business for 2 miles. Our loss was heavy—but Genl Grant's was much heavier. I lost six killed in my little Co., & was slightly wounded myself. Genl Grant began his march to the right in the direction of Spottsylvania. Had heavy skirmishing along the line until we got to Spottsylvania. We stormed the town & took it. A few days later fought the battle of the Horsehoe or Spottsylvania. Genl Gordon often said this was the hardest battle of the war. Our loss was heavy. I lost six killed in a little while.

Our next battle was at Cold Harbour June 3, 1864, and it was a hard one. Genl Grant's loss was awful as they had done the charging. Hiss loss from May 6th to June 3d was estimated at over 60,000.

We had considerable marching, skirmishing on the north side of the James River. Our next battle was at the Crator at Petersburg & then a good many skirmishes & battles around Petersburg & then on the retreat fighting incessantly until the wind up at Appomatox.

The following is copied from W. R. Montgomery's Daily
Pocket Remembrancer *for 1863.*[1]

Jan 1 — Thursday — **1863**. In camp near Falmouth. A
Great Streak of Luck. Drinking Rum, running horse
races & a foot race for a purse of ten dollars. Big thing.
New Years Day.

Jan. 2 — Friday — Martin Norton, No. 70 Green Street,
Jersey City.
Catharine Lyons, 84 Essex Street, Jersey City.

Jan. 7 — Yorktown, Williams Bridge, Seven Pines, Fair
Oaks, Battle on the 25th at the Oaks — seven days
before Richmond, Malvern Hill 2nd.

Jan. 8 — Bristow Station, Bull Run 2nd, Chantitto (?),
Fredricksburg, Stafford C.H. Was our first appearance
into Virginia.

Jan. 10 — South Street, between Second & Lombard
Sts., Shades, Bernard Keaman.

Jan. 12 — Boston Post, 1 Kistleburg x 2 Mills x — 3
Elliot x — 4   Taylor   x — 5   Hughes   x — 6   Beleah — 7
Bellah — 8 Carter — 9 Ritch — 10 Howard x — 11 Haton
x — 12 Manning x — 13 Barratt — 13 in all.

Jan. 18 — 163 Reg New York Vol, Consolidated with
the F...(illeg) 73rd Reg NY vols.

---

[1] These first entries, through March 20, are a handwriting later than
the rest of the diary and give a summary of WRM's role in the war.

Jan 20 — Appointed Sargt. between this date & the 22nd January by lieut Ramsey by orders signed J. Salmon.

Feb. 1 — Sunday — All hands stinking drunk.

Feb. 2 — Monday — On Guard the 1st — Relief Officer of the Day Lieut Hardey.

Feb. 3 — Received a letter from sister Bridget and answered it.

Feb. 5 — Left camp marching in light rain. Marched all day in snow & rain. Camped in the woods at night.

Feb. 6, 1863 — Struck tents. Marched on again — within one mile of Rapahanick Bridge, rested all day & dryed our clothes. At night we started back 3 miles.

Feb. 7 — We woke up with our shoes all frozen, thawed them out & started for the camp the distance of 16 miles, reached camp well played out.

Feb. 8 — Everything quiet & whiskey in the Bargen.

Feb. 9 — Fine day but very muddy under foot.

Feb. 11 — On Fatigue Duty.

Feb. 12 — Recd a letter from Sister Bridget & answered it on the spot.

Feb. 13 — Recd a letter from John Donnelly & answered it. Sent one to Father.
Recd a paper from Bridget. Mike Harvey started for New York.

Feb. 14—Visited by Thomas Gartlin (?) with the Counter Sign—The Cock Crew & the ball opened the more ...(illeg.) for the day.

Feb. 15—On Guard. Capt Puetell Officer of the Day. Lieut Hardye Officer of the Guard 3d Relief Corpl Penn C.H. Raining.

Feb. 16—Jack Lee visited the Fire Tan...(illeg.) On or about Camp near Falmouth, Va. with his Haver Sack full of Jumbles & Cheeses. Bully for Jack.

Feb. 17—Snowing hard.

Feb. 18—Recd a letter from Sister Bridget and answered it this day. Jack Lee started for his camp. Raining hard.

Feb. 21, 1863—Recd a letter from Bridget & answered this date. Johnny Moore was to see us.

Feb. 22—The Reg gone on Picket. Snowing hard all day & night.

Feb. 23—Fine day. Plenty of snow on the ground.

Feb. 24—Fair day. Prity sharp wind.

Feb. 25—Recd a letter from Sister Bridget & answered on the spot.

Feb. 28, 1863—Mustered for pay by Col. Brewerton. Mike Langan started for New York, a citizen once more.

March 1 — On guard the 2nd Relief.

Mar. 2 — Lt. Rollan, Co. D 3 New York, five graves of New York Volunteers.

Mar. 3 — Recd two letters, one from father & one from Sister Bridget. Answered both on this date.

March 4 — Left my pants to be altered with Fitzpatrick.

Mar. 7 — A tree fell in camp & killed a member of Co G named James Murry of Brooklyn.

Mar. 8 — Received a letter from Sister Bridget & answered it this date at camp near Falmouth Va.

Mar. 11 — Received a letter from Mike Langan and answered it on the spot.

Mar. 13 — On Guard 1st Relief Corp Lappson Hardy Office of the Day. Tye Officer of the Guard.

Mar. 17 — I went to the races at Irish Blockade. Recd a letter from Sister Bridget & answered it on the spot. Heavy firing on the right.

Mar. 19 — Wrote to J. Donnelly this morning.

Mar. 20 — A man can gain nothing in the company of the N.C.Vols. Beware how you speak of an ...?

Mar. 21 — Started off On Picket. Snowing. Lieut Ramsey went home on furlough. Sarg of the Second Relief Corp Lapp...

Mar. 22—On Picket over on the Reserve.

Mar. 23—...(illeg.) On Picket yet. Everything quiet along the lines.

Mar. 24—Started back for Camp & arrived safe.

Mar. 26—Recd a letter from Sister Bridget of the 22nd Sunday.

Mar. 27, 1863 —We were to the Races over at Berrys Head Quarters. The day was favorable & everything passed off bully. I recd a letter from J. Donnelly of the 22nd.

Mar. 28, 1863—I received a letter from Q. P. Langan of the 22 inst.[2]

Apr. 28—We started from Camp about 4 O Clk. Marched a short distance, camped in the woods.

Apr. 29—Packed up our Danage (?) & started a short distance further & camped in the woods. Raining this eavng.

Apr. 30, 1863—Laying still in the woods. Raining.

May 30—The Regt was payed off today at Camp Ellen Va.

---

[2] In the March 29 space, daily handwritten entries by W. R. Montgomery begin. A few items in the former handwriting are scattered in later pages; some pages are blank, one is cut out. The few other entries in the earlier handwriting are given below.

Entries made in Daily Pocket Remembrances for 1863.[3]

July — Monday 6 — 1863 — Marched all day. Arrived at Hagerstown near night. Camped about two miles from town on the Sharpsburg Road. *Had no rations since the day before.*

Tuesday 7 — Went about one mile down the road on picket. Was relieved by Gen Kershaw. Then marched towards Williamsport. Camped below about two miles.

Wednesday 8 — Woke up this morning wet, was raining. *Rained all day. No tents. Slept on a bundle of wheat and covered with an oil cloth. Had a good supper — fried chicken.*

Thursday 9 — Went last night with four men to guard an old man's Bee Gums. Gave us a good breakfast. Returned to camp soon after. Had a very good dinner. Dr. Hardy ate with us. Nothing new going on in camp. I am now going to bed.

July 1863 — Friday 10 — Nothing unusual in camp today. Had a prettie heavy cavalry fight in our front. The Yanks drove us back. We were ordered into line, but were not called out. Stacked arms & are going to sleep.

Saturday 11 — Our Battalion was sent out to find the position of the Yankie. Was skirmishing all day.

---

[3] Dates are printed in booklet, three spaces to a page. The first part of the booklet has entries by another soldier. Then, with dates changed in ink, there are 1864 entries by W. R. Montgomery.

Our loss in the Batt some six or sever killed, wounded & missing.

Sunday 12—Nothing of interest today. Lay in camp all day. Heard of the fall of Vicksburg. Received three letters from home (sister Em, Misses Lou & Lila). Skirmishing in front all day. Heavy rain. No tents.

Monday 13—Was out skirmishing all day. Had a prettie tight little fight. About dark the Yankies drove us back. Our army began to fall back about dark. We remained until daylight.

Tuesday 14—Crossed the Potomac on a Pontoon Bridge about 12 o'clock. Gen A.P.Hill had a little fight. Took 300 prisoners (cavalry). Gen Petagrew was killed. Camped 6 miles from Martinsburg.

Wednesday 15—Took up our march again toward Winchester. The road was very muddy. Camped at Bunkershill—11 miles from Winchester. *Had no rations. Drew 1/2 lb flour the night before & ate it up immediately. Going to sleep.*

Thursday 16—Remained in camp all day. Cooked two days ration. Saw Bill Dane. No news today. Wrote to Mother.

Friday 17—Still in camp at Bunkershill. Rained all day. No news. Saw a letter from Miss M—M.

Saturday 18—Nothing new today. Moved camp this evening to a beautiful grove about two miles from Bunkers Hill.

Sunday 19—Nothing new today. Rev. Mr. Crinly (?) of Augusta preached. I was officer of the Guard, could not attend. Wrote a letter to Sister Emma.

Monday 20—Left Bunkers Hill this morning 6 o'clock. Camped tonight at Millwood. No news in camp today. Had a hard march.

Tuesday 21—Left Millwood this morning. Marched all day up the Shenandoah river. Crossed on pontoons about 10 o'clock. Camped near Front Royal on the mountains. *Had no rations nor blanket.*

July 1863—Wednesday 22—Marched through Front Royal & on across the mountains. Got on top the mountain 12 o'clock. Passed Pickets Division. Had a fight with the Yankie Calvary. Captured 36 Beeves & drove them back. Slept on the mountain.

Thursday 23—Left the mountains at daylight for Gain's X road. Cooked rations & started out for Culpepper (20). Camped on the Hazel River 10 miles form Culpepper Court House.

Friday 24—Passed through Culpepper about 12 o'clock. Camped 2 miles from town on the Fredricksburg road. Cooked two days rations.

Saturday 25—Still at Culpepper. Remained in camp all day. Had Brigade Inspection at 6 o'clock. Wrote a letter Home, also one to Miss Lula Boyd. My last letter to her I suppose.

Sunday 26—Remained in camp all day. No news of interest. Our Brigade was inspected by Gen Longstreet at 9 o'clock. Henry came in from Stanton. Had not seen him since left Md.

Monday 27—Nothing new in camp today. Wrote a letter to Aunt Frank & Sister Em. Had a heavy rain.

Tuesday 28—Nothing going on in camp today. Went to Culpepper today. Bought segars & cakes. Came up a heavy rain.

Wednesday 29—Nothing new in camp today. Had Brigade Inspection at 8 o'clock by Lt. Hacket. Had a heavy rain today again. Went to preaching tonight, Rev. Mr. Blanton preached.

Thursday 30—Nothing interesting again in camp today. No letter from Home yet. Haven't heard from Home since the 12 of July.

Friday 31—*(Illeg., too soft a pencil, something about orders to be ready to move.)*

August 1—Saturday—Was ready to leave at appointed hour. Order was countermanded. Lay on line all day expecting Yankies. No news in camp.

Sunday 2—Still lying in camp ready to leave at any hour. Had preaching. Received a letter from Sister Em. Was glad to hear from home. No news today.

Monday 3—Received orders to march about 9 o'clock. It was awful hot. Marched from

August 1863—Monday 3 continuied—Culpepper by Slaughter Mt. to Rapidan River. Crossed about 9 o'clock below the R. R. Bridge.

Tuesday 4—Remained in camp all day. In the evening went in swimming. No news today. Very hot indeed.

Wednesday 5—Left camp at 9 o'clock this morning. Took up our march towards Fredricksburg. Camped about 10 miles from Chancellorsville. No news today. Very hot.

Thursday 6—After breakfast this morning I crawled in my little tent & went to sleep. Slept until dinner. No news today. Had a nice mess of beans for supper.

Friday 7—No news today. All quiet. Wrote a letter to Sister Em. Rained all day.

Saturday 8—Moved camp today about one mile. Received a letter from Sister Emma today. No news today of interest. Very warm indeed.

Sunday 9—Lay in camp all day. Dr. Styles preached about two miles from here. Did not hear it in time to go. Took a good bath.

Monday 10—No news in camp today. I was officer of the guard today. Wrote a letter home.

Tuesday 11—Nothing unusual in camp today. Was on drill this morning & Evening. Wrote a letter to Mr. J. T. Haley at Chattanooga, Tenn.

Wednesday 12—Lay in camp all day with the exception of morning & evening drills. Very warm indeed today. No letters as usual form Home or any where else.

Thursday 13 — Woke up this morning it was raining. Rained hard all day. I had to keep quite close all day in my little bivouac.

Friday 14 — Lay in camp all day. No news today. Very warm. Went in swimming this evening.

Saturday 15 — All quiet today. No news. No drills today. Wash day.

Sunday 16 — Had inspection this morning at 8 1/2 o'clock. Several young ladies were present.

August 1863 — Monday 17 — Heavy cannonading in the direction of Fredricksburg. Rec'd orders to be ready to move. Henry came in from Orange Court House. Heard of the death of Mrs. R. T. Glover. All quiet tonight.

Tuesday 18 — No news today. Received no letters from home. Genl Inspection & Review by Maj Genl McLaws.

Wednesday 19 — Wrote a letter home. Lay in camp all day.

Thursday 20 — No news today. Received a letter form Mother & answered it immediately.

Friday 21 — Today is fast day. Had a sermon from the Rev. Mr. Doll, Chaplain of the 18th Geo. Vols.

Saturday 22 — Struck tents this morning at daylight. Marched about 23 miles in the area of Louisa Court House. Gave $5 for two small water melons.

Sunday 23 — Took up our march again at daylight. Marched about 10 miles & camped at Good Hope Church, in an old field. I was officer of the Guard.

Monday 24 — I went out foraging today. Staid all night 10 miles from camp near New Market.

Tuesday 25 — Returned to camp. Rec'd orders to move about five miles. Had a good supper. Cos Sam & Lt. Windsor ate with us. Had fried chicken & butter.

Wednesday 26 — Moved camp today about five miles, near Wallers Tavern on the East Anna River. Have a beautiful camp. Hen Came in R — .

Thursday 27 — No news in camp today. Henry went to Richmond today. I wrote two letters, one to Sister Em & one to Mother. Had water melon.

Friday 28 — Nothing of interest occurred today. had an excellent dinner, Apple Dumplings with sugar & butter sauce.

(Page missing)

September 1863 — Friday 4 — No news today in camp.

Saturday 5 — Nothing unusual in camp today.

Septmber 1863 — Sunday 6 — Received a letter from home. I was officer of the guard today.

Monday 7 — Had Division Inspection today at 10 o'clock. Wrote a letter to Sister Em.

Tuesday 8—Struck tents about daylight & marched to Beaverdam Station to take the cars, but had to march to Hanover Junction, a distance of 25 or 26 miles.

Wednesday 9—Lay in camp all day waiting for the train, but it did not come. Expect to leave tomorrow.

Thursday 10—Left camp this morning for Hanover Junction, 3 miles, for the cars. The Brigade could not all go at once. I left with the 16th & 19th Geo Regts. Staid in R— at Soldier Geo Home.

Friday 11—Staid last night at Soldier Home with Dr. Groves & Henry. The Battalion came in about two o'clock. Strolled about over town until 8 o'clock, then all aboard for Petersburg.

Saturday 12—Arrived at Petersburg about 2 o'clock A.M. Staid there until 9 o'clock P.M. Then left for Weldon, N. C. Arrived at Weldon at daylight.

Sunday 13—Arrived at Weldon, N. C. about daylight & started immediately for Wilmington & arrived there about dark. Had a good supper at the City Hotel, Wilmington.

Monday 14—Left Wilmington Monday night for Kingsville, So.Ca. Travelled all night.

Tuesday 15—Arrived at Florence, So.Ca., about 10 o'clock & arrived at Kingsville So.Ca. about 10 o'clock P.M. Left immediately for Augusta.

Wednesday 16—Arrived at Augusta at 1 o'clock & remained there until dark & then left for Atlanta, Geo.

Thursday 17—Arrived at Atlanta, Geo. about dark. Met Mother & Sister at the cars. Went out Home & staid all night.

Friday 18—Remained in Atlanta all day. Saw Carrie & Mary Rall. Took supper at Uncle Deans.

September 1863—Saturday 19—Left Atlanta, Geo., at 8 o'clock. Passed through Marietta, did not stop. Saw Miss Lou. Would have given a small negro to have stopped but could not.

Sunday 20—Arrived at Ringgold last night. No rations. Marched on from R— about 6 miles & camped. Like to froze. Gen Hood was wounded. Drove the Yankies back.

Monday 21—Took up our march before day & moved on to the field. Saw Gens Bragg & Polk & Breckinridge. The Yanks fell back. Took a large amt. of artillery.

Tuesday 22—Followed on after the Yanks some 6 miles. At the foot of Lookout Mt. had a heavy skirmish. D. Richardson of our com was killed. Drove the Yanks back.

Wednesday 23—All has been quiet today except now & then a few shells from the Yankies. Wrote a letter home. No news. Saw B. Green just from home. Had a message from Miss Lou.

Thursday 24—Was woke up this morning rather earlier than usual by the Yankies shell. Had a heavy skirmish. Drove the Yanks back. About 10 o'clock advanced & had a hot skirmish.

Friday 25—In front all day. Nothing new. Short rations again today.

Saturday 26—Sent out a squad to feel the Yankies. Had a hot skirmish, five or six wounded. Saw J. T. Haley. Went round last night to see the Layden Artillery. Saw J. A. Kilby.

Sunday 27—All quiet today. The Yanks sent us a flag of truce, a dispatch to Gen Bragg. The flag remained from 10 o'clock A.M. to 4 P.M. Could not learn what the truce was for. I am quite unwell.

Monday 28—A negro was shot last night by our videts. A flag of truce was up again. Yanks sent in for their wounded. A long train of ambulances. No news today. All quiet.

Tuesday 29—All quiet in front today. We have been on duty for 8 days. Short rations. Yankees carried about 1000 wounded through our lines. A flag of truce was up all day.

Wednesday 30—Was relieved from the front today. Have been on 9 days. Visited the Laden Artillery. Saw J. Haynes, J. Kilby & Tyler Cooper. Came up a rain, Saw Gov. Brown & Gen Bragg.

October 1863—Thursday 1—Remained in camp all day. Rained hard all day. No news in camp today.

Friday 2—Nothing of interest today. Lt. Barrratt visited the top of Lookout Mountain. Had a visit from J.A.Haynes. Wrote a letter to Mother.

Saturday 3—All quiet on front today. Capt. Gober has been quite sick. Confined to his bed all day.

Sunday 4—Nothing unusual has occurred today. I visited the Layden Artillery, also the old 2nd SoCa Vols. Saw many of my old friends.

Monday 5—Capt. Gober was quite sick. Left today for the hospital. Nothing of interest today. A cannonading was kept up all day by both sides.

Tuesday 6— No news today again. Heard that Miss Lou & Capt. Williams were soon to be married.

Wednesday 7—Today was election day for Gov. I voted for Gov. Brown, Geo N. Lester, Calhoun, Green & Gartrell. No letter again from home today.

Thursday 8—No news again today. Saw Ellis Hull. Came to our camp.

Friday 9—No news today. Still in camp.

Saturday 10—Made out pay & Muster Rolls today & paid the Co off. All quiet in front.

Sunday 11—Had Brigade Inspection Gen Wofford. No news from home yet. All quiet in front.

Monday 12—Had Brigade Inspection by Maj Coskins. Heavy firing below Chattanooga.

Tuesday 13—Rained all day & is still raining.

Wednesday 14—No news today. Rained all day. Got wet last night. *Wrote a letter home.*

Thursday 15—Still raining. Got wet again last night.

Friday 16—All quiet in front today. Received a letter form Capt Gober. Heard that Miss Lou Boyd was married the 10th 1861.

(No entries October 1863—17 and 18)

Monday 19—Raining yet. Received a letter form home, first in a month. Also received a letter from Capt. Gober. Heard that Henry was coming up to see me.

Tuesday 20—Borrowed an old mule & started out to meet Henry. Went to Chickamauga Station & from there to Tiner's (?) Station but no Henry. Returned to camp hungry & worn out.

Wednesday 21—No news today. All quiet in front. Rained again today.

Thursday 22—Received a letter from Aunt Frank, also one from Capt Gober. Heard Miss Lou Boyd was married on the 18th. No news form home. Almost starved for something good to eat.

Friday 23—Rained all day. Had to stay in my little old tent, wrapped up in my blankets to keep warm. Wrote a letter to N. N. G.

Saturday 24—Heavy cannonading below on the River. Ellis Hull came over & took dinner with us.

Sunday 25—No news in camp today. Slept all day. Ellis Hull staid all night with us on his way to Quincy, Fla. Had chicken for breakfast, also honey.

Monday 26—Visited the Layden Artillery. Saw J. Haynes & Jim Kilby. Received a letter from Sister Em.

Tuesday 27—All quiet today. Had orders for drill twice a day. Heard an order also for one of Phillips Legion (Co E) to be shot.

Wednesday 28—Had Inspection today by Lt Young. Received three letters from home—one from Sister, one from Dr. G. & one from Miss Eliza.

Thursday 29—Was called up this morning at 2 o'clock. Marched about 3 miles through mud knee deep. Stopped at daylight at the foot of Lookout Mt. Had a hard fight on the other side of the Mt. Wrote to Sister.

Friday 30—Woke up last night & it was raining. Had no tents. Had to take the rain as it came. Rained steady all day.

Saturday 31—Still raining. Has rained all day. Spent an awful night last night. Was quite cold. Moved camp today at the foot of Lookout Mt. Have no tents yet.

November 1863—Sunday 1—Today has been a beautiful day. Got our tents today. Fixed up our beds, Sunday as it was. Worked hard all day. Henry came in form home. Brought some good things, but left them at the depot.

Monday 2—Received my box today. Had a good time. Had Opossum, Chicken, Potatoes, Butter, peach pies & some oh! such nice apples. Like to hurt myself eating.

Tuesday 3—No news in camp today. Lay in camp & ate Butter & Potatoes all day. Jim Kilby & John Haynes ate supper with me last night. I wrote a letter home to Sister.

Wednesday 4— Received orders last night to send back tents & all we could not carry & be ready to leave at daylight.

Thursday 5—4th—Remained in camp all day. Saw W. J. Kilby just from home. Took a turkey with Jim Kilby & John Haynes. 5th—Left camp last night for Chickamauga Station to take the cars.

Friday 6—Took the cars at Chickamauga Station last night. Remained all night. Left this morning for Sweetwater, Tenn. Arrived here at night. Marched about one mile & struck camp.

Saturday 7—Remained in camp all day. The Boys were all out foraging all day. Brought in hogs, sheep, geese, chickens & cabbage in abundance. We are nearly killing ourselves eating.

Sunday 8—Still in camp near Sweetwater. We are living high. Boys all enjoying themselves fine. Made an exchange with Dr. Herring for Dr. Enfort of the 42d Geo.

Monday 9—Moved camp today, across the R.R. about one mile from Sweetwater. Bob Wood came in from Marietta. Dr. Gober has not come yet. Am looking for him daily.

Tuesday 10—Still in camp near Sweetwater. Henry started for home today but ain't got off. Will go tomorrow.[4]

Thursday 12—Moved camp about 6 miles from Sweetwater near Philadelphia on R.R. Went out foraging. Bought some cabbage & molasses. Had orders to move at daylight.

Friday 13—Marched hard all day. Camped on the river near Morgantown, 7 miles form Louden. Went about 4 miles foraging. Bought chickens & got dinner. Had orders to move at 12 o'clock.

Saturday 14—Commenced our march at the appointed hour. Marched to Louden. It is very hard marching, very dark. Got to Louden before day. Lay in an old field. Hoods Division crossed the River. Camped near Louden. Gen Hoods Division crossed the river in the evening. We will cross tomorrow.

Sunday 15—Crossed the River soon this morning. Marched about 8 miles from Louden, near the Yankies.

Monday 16—Took up our march again soon this morning. Came upon the Yankies in the evening. Had a prettie hard fight. Drove them back. Slept on the field.

---

[4] No entry for 11th. Dates printed in booklet are changed for a few entries.

Tuesday 17—Marched on today again. Overtook the Yankies 5 miles from Knoxville. Drove them on. Had another fight 3 miles from K— & drove them in again & are now in camp 5 miles from K—.

Wednesday 18—Was out skirmishing all day. Gen Kershaw's Brigade charged the Y—out of breast works. We have very short rations now. No bread today & no meat for the last 3 days. We are in sight of Knoxville, Tenn.

Thursday 19—Advanced our skirmish line. Was skirmishing all day. We have the enemy surrounded. We are living on short rations, less than half.

Friday 20—Still in front. The Yankies last night burned up a good many houses in K—. Heavy skirmishing all day. One man wounded, Corp. Beacham Co D.

Saturday 21—Rained all night. I was on front line. Had to take it all day & last night too. Heavy skirmishing all day. Nobody hurt on our side. Was relieved by Cobb's Legion.

Sunday 22—Had to go in front again today. Capt. Gober came in from home today. Received two letters from home, also my overcoat. No news. Received a letter from Aunt Frank.

Monday 23—Our Bat was relieved again last night. No news. I wrote a letter to Sister Em.

Tuesday 24—Went on front line again today. The 2nd Michigan charged & flanked our works. Drove us back for a while, but we soon drove them back. Killed & wounded a great many. Our loss was 5 wounded. (N.H.Stewart from our Co.)

November 1863 — Wednesday 25 — Sharp skirmishing all day. No news from home. Was relieved from picket by the 16th Geo Regt. Read a letter from a Yankie Lady to her sweetheart, Agt Noble who was killed yesterday.

Thursday 26 — Visited Gen Kershaws Brigade today. Saw the Palmetto Guards. Heard of Gen Johnson Div coming to reinforce us. Saw all the Yankies buried & graves marked.

Friday 27 — Went back to hospital & made a coffin for N. H. Stewart, who died last night from wounds received on the 24th. Saw a great many Yankies wounded.

Saturday 28 — Rained all day. Had quite a disagreeable tine on front line.

Sunday 29 — Charged the Yankies fortifications. Climed the works. Had to fall back. Col Ruff & Capt Johnson was killed & many others. Our loss was heavy.

Monday 30 — Was relieved from the front last night. Went to the rear for the first time since we came here. Read a novel all day (Esparanza or The Home of the Wanderers).

December 1863 — Tuesday 1 — Remained in camp all day. Had Inspection by Lt. Hacket. Wrote a letter to Sister Emma. Had to go on front lines again at dark. No news from home.

Wednesday 2—Remained on front line all day. Was relieved at dark by the 16th Geo Regt & Cobb's Geo Legion.

Thursday 3—Went out to the wagons to change clothes as our wagons had come in from Louden. Had orders to cook 4 days rations & be ready to leave at any time. Saw J. E. Kilby.

Friday 4—Remained in camp all day ready to leave at a moments notice. Had election for Maj. & Ranking Capt. Capt. Gober was elected Maj &c.

Saturday 5—Marched all night. Halted at daylight to rest for a while. Had to wade a creek. Was awful cold. Had a hard time marching. Saw the old 2nd S. C. Vols.

Sunday 6—After a good nights rest, we again took up our march. Marched all day. Roads quite muddy. Was very tired at night. Camped in 2 miles of Rutlage Tenn.

Monday 7—Lay in camp all day waiting for the Yankies. No news. Bought some apples at $4.00 per Dz. We are now in a Union county.

December 1863—Tuesday 8—Took up our march again today, in the direction of Bristol. Marched all day. Was quite tired at night. Camped near Bean Station at night.

Wednesday 9—Started again soon this morning. Camped near Rogersville. Very tired at night. No rations at all. Nearly starved for something to eat.

Thursday 10—Remained in Camp all day. Drew 1/2 lb four per man. All nearly starved for something to eat. Wrote to Sister Emma. Had a chance to send it by Adjt Porter Cobb's Geo Legion.

Friday 11—Here we are in the wilderness about 50 miles from Bristol, 8 miles from Rogersville near the Holston River & about 15 miles from nowhere, between 2 mountains.

Saturday 12—Still in the wilderness. Rained all evening. We living on half rations & it goes very hard. Was nearly all day making hominy. Change clothes today for the first time in a month.

Sunday 13—Went on horseback to look for the Layden Artillery but couldn't find it. Met Gen Gracy's Brigade. Short rations yet. Drew one ear of corn to the man. Got orders to be ready to move at daylight.

Monday 14—Left camp at daylight. Marched towards Knoxville. Came on the Yanks at Bean Station. Drove them back. Took a great many wagons. No rations at all today.

Tuesday 15—Slept last night at the camp fires built by the Yankies. Had no blankets. Slept quite cold. Moved up the valley about one mile, across the Cumberland Gap Road.

Wednesday 16—No rations yet. Ate the last I had for dinner yesterday. Don't know when I will get any more. Am almost starved. Hello, I hear we are to draw 2 days full rations, *good, good.*

Thursday 17—Moved camp today about 3 1/2 miles from Cumberland Gap Road. Had a good breakfast on beef & bread. We have been starved for 4 or 5 days. Col H is in comd of Brigade.

Friday 18—Today was very cold. We are camped on a mountain. Dr. Gober bought a turkey & a ham. Will have a good supper if nothing happens. Gen McLaws has been relieved of his command (today).

December 1863—Saturday 19—Very cold yet. Heard today that we were to move to mountains to build winter quarters. We are now living finely. Had for dinner today—pork, hominy & nice biscuit. Haven't heard from home in over 6 weeks.

Sunday 20—Marched today at 1 o'clock past Bean Station towards Morristown & marched to the river about 8 miles. Camped for the night. I am very cold. Will cross the river today, I suppose in a flat boat.

Monday 21—Took up our march again about dark. Crossed the river in a flat boat. Moved at one (?) ... (illeg.) was until 12 o'clock at night crossing. Camped about one mile from the river. Had a good fire.

Tuesday 22—Took up our march again today. Marched about 4 miles. Cross the R. R. at Russellville about 60 miles form Bristol. Camped for the night. Will move tomorrow for Winter Qrtrs.

Wednesday 23—Spent the day in camp. Col Hutchins selected this spot for our Winter Qrtrs. Late this evening laid off a camp. Cut some logs to build me a hut.

Thursday 24—Worked hard all day on my little cabin. Will finish tomorrow if nothing happens., My hands are quite sore from using the ax.

Friday 25—7 o'clock P.M. (*night*) spent my Christmas today in building a chimney to my hut. Worked hard all day & am now sitting by a good fire enjoying the fruits of my labor.

Saturday 26—Today it rained. Spent my time in fixing up my hut.

Sunday 27—Spent today in lying about camp. Had a good dinner, apple rolls, backbone & biscuit. Took a ride over to the 2nd So Ca Vols. Wrote a letter to Sister.

Monday 28—Went out to get a private room for Capt Gober who is quite sick. Found him a nice room at Mrs. Bouce's. Had him taken over in an ambulance.

Tuesday 29—Went to see Capt. Gober today. Found him much better. Returned to camp to fix up my hut.

Wednesday 30—Went again today to see Capt Gober & found him much better. No news in camp. Am anxiously looking forward to a furlough. We are living finely now.

Thursday 31—The last day of the year 63. Went to see Capt Gober again. He is much better. I am now in a hut & mess alone. Have a good old time.

January 1864—Friday 1—Today has indeed been a cold one. I went to Capt Gober today. He is improving. Had oh! such a nice dinner to at Mrs. Bouce's. Oh it is awful cold & the poor soldiers are almost naked.

Saturday 2—Nothing unusual in camp today. Very cold. My furlough came back disapproved. Was sorry I assure you. I will try again.

Sunday 3—Payson Ardis left today for home on 30 days furlough. Wrote a letter by him. Wish I could have gone with him. Very cold yet. It is now snowing.

Monday 4—*(blank)*

Tuesday 5—No news in camp today. Went over & took dinner with cos Sam & Bill. Had a nice supper. Had ham, biscuit & brains.

Wednesday 6—Woke up this morning & found the ground covered in snow. It is quite cold. No news from home. Sam Manget came over & staid all night. Had a good time.

Thursday 7—Snow is still on the ground & is very cold. Capt Gober is yet sick.

Friday 8—Snow is yet on the ground & oh it is awful cold. Lay in camp all day by a good fire.

Saturday 9—Went over to see Capt Gober today. He is much better. Was able to be over at camp.

Sunday 10—Today has been indeed quiet though quite cold. Snow on the ground yet.
I remained in camp all day. Col approved my furlough.

Monday 11 — Everything is very quiet except now & then a little chicken fighting. Dr. Gober went before the board today to get a sick furlough.

Tuesday 12 — *(blank)*

Wednesday 13[5]

Thursday 14 — Made out Pay rolls for the camp & paid them off. My furlough came back disapproved. Was very sorry as I am quite anxious to go home.

Friday 15 — Received orders last night at midnight to cook rations & be ready to leave at daylight. It was quite cold. Snow on the ground. March as far as Morristown & camped for the night.

Saturday 16 — Lay in the woods all day near Morristown. It was quite cold. Heard heavy firing of artillery late in the evening. I am almost barefooted. My foot is on the ground.

(In space for 13th) Look in the beginning of this Book for continuation of this diary. See March 29th 63 for Jan the 17th 64 &c.[6]

Sunday 17 — Lay in the woods all day near Morristown awaiting orders. It is quite cold. Snow on the ground & I am almost bare — footed.

---

[5] Blank, except for memorandum which follows the entry of the 16th below.

[6] On the next three pages are a mixture of accounts for Mess No. 1, with various amounts due Capt N. N.Gober, W. R.Montgomery, and Barrett, and memos of items bought: Water Mellon, Apples, Flour, Soap, Syrup, Milk …(illeg). The only non — mess item is: John II — V.

Monday 18 — Received orders about dark to return to camp. The roads are quite muddy & it was also quite cold. Got camp about 9 o'clock. Had a heavy snow. Received a letter.

Tuesday 19 — Remained in Camp all day. The ground is covered in snow & my shoes were too bad to be out. Heard today that Capt. Johnson was not dead.

Wednesday 20 — Visited Capt. G— again today. Took a ride on horseback. Returned to Camp & wrote a letter to Sister & sent it by Jos. T. Lowrey. No news from home yet.

Thursday 21 — Went over to see Capt Gober. Also took a ride on horseback to Russellville for some whiskey for Capt. G. Lt Barratt received a trunk of clothes.

Friday 22 — Nothing doing in camp today. Wrote a letter to Aunt Narcissa. Haven't heard from home in two months (today).

Sunday 24 — Remained in Camp all day. No letters from home yet. Haven't heard from Home since Nov. the 23rd 1863.

Tuesday 26 — Was all day at the shoe shop having my shoes mended. Got them very nicely fixed at last.

Wednesday 27 — Remained in Camp all day. No news from home yet. Sent up a furlough but am afraid I will not get for such is my luck.

January 1864 — Thursday 28 — Went over & staid with Capt Gober last night. Had a good breakfast. Capt. left for home. Went back to camp. Had orders to move at 12 o'clock. Marched to near Morristown.

Thursday 28 — I received a letter from a young lady signed "Viola Boyd" (Leap Year). Never heard of her before.

Friday 29 — Had a hard march. Camped in four miles of Morristown last night. Got up this morning & marched at 3 o'clock. Had a rough time. Very sore feet indeed. Passed through Dandridge.

Saturday 30 — Camped last night in 6 miles of Dandridge. Remained there until late in the evening when we marched back toward D. Camped in about 2 miles of that place.

Sunday 31 — Took up our march quite early to camp. Marched hard. Got to camp an hour by sun. Almost worn out. Marched about 25 miles.

February 1864 — Monday 1 — Lay in camp all day resting after our long walk of yesterday. I am very sore yet. Went to the Qrtr Master & drew a Pr of Shoes.

Tuesday 2 — Woke up soon this morning & wrote a letter to Miss "Viola". Had company drill at 10 o'clock A.M.

Wednesday 3 — Today has been quite cold. Had a hard storm last night. Drew clothing from Geo. All got supplied well. Plenty of shoes & pants & jackets.

Thursday 4—Had Inspection today. Was quite cold & windy. Wrote a letter to Sister Emma. Have not heard from Home since Nov. the 27th 1863. W.D.Anderson is quite sick.

Friday 5—Went over to see Bill Anderson. Found him quite sick with Pneumonia but a little easier this evening. My furlough came a few minutes ago all O. K. Will leave tomorrow for Geo.

Saturday 6—Went again to see Bill Anderson. Found him much better. Left camp today at one o'clock P.M. to take the cars for home.

Sunday 7—Took cars at Russellville at 9 o'clock A.M. & arrived at Bristol at 6 o'clock P.M. Had a very good time tonight. Apples & pies in abundance.

Monday 8—Left Bristol at 1 o'clock A.M. & arrived at Lynchburg Va. at 6 P.M. & left immediately for Petersburg.

February 1864 —Tuesday 9—Arrived at Petersburg at 7 o'clock A.M. & left immediately for Weldon. Arrived at Weldon at 4 P.M. & left for Wilmington soon after.

Wednesday 10—Arrived at Wilmington at daylight & took the cars immediately for Kingsville. Engine broke down & had to lay over all night.

Thursday 11—Arrived at Kingsville just in time to be too late. Will lose 24 hours in getting home.

(**NOTE**: *No entries in the Daily Pocket Remembrances for 1864 made by W. R. Montgomery from Feb. 11, 1864, until* *that of July 6, 1864, but the diary is continued in a small memo book with the following inscription on the fly leaf.)*

> W. R. Montgomery
> Co F 3d Bat Geo S.S.
> Woffords Brigade
> McLaw's Division
> Longstreet's Corps
> Greenville
> Tenn

Bought in Augusta Geo. March 7, 1864

Greenville Tenn[7]

Sunday, March 13th 1864—Went over to see Capt Harris of Phillips Legion. Received orders to be ready to march at daylight.

Monday 14—Left camp at sunrise this morning for Bull's Gap & camped about 2 miles form Midway.

Tuesday 15—Left Midway at daylight & crossed Lick Creek on the R.R. Bridge. *Very cold.* Marched about 4 miles & formed line of battle to wait for the Yankies.

Wednesday 16—Still in the woods. It is awful cold. Slept last night on the side of a hill, like to have frozen. We had a little snow.

Thursday 17—Co F had to go on picket. All quiet in front.

March 1864—Friday 18—Was relieved from Picket today by Co A S.S.

---

[7] In pencil, the rest of the entry in ink.

Saturday 19—No news, all quiet. Short ration of "Graham flour". Received orders about dark to return to camp 18 miles. Marched very hard and arrived in camp about 11 o'clock at night quite tired. Ate my three days in one day. Will have to do without till Tuesday night.

Sunday 20—Went to preaching today. Heard Mr. Yarbrough preach.

Monday 21—Moved camp today. Had Brigade Inspection. Went with P. L. Ardis to see some of his lady friends. Had a huge time. Pace took on considerably with Miss Ellen, but I stood off & looked on. Got back at 9 o'clock.

Tuesday 22—Woke up this morning & found it snowing very heavy. It is now about knee deep & still snowing hard. We are now drawing only half rations of flour brand & all & the dirtiest stuff you heard of or saw. Boys all went to Gen Wofford last night for rations. Said they were suffering & rations they would have. Gen made a short speech. Made fair promises to them, to some extent pacified them & had an extra days rations issued about 12 o'clock at night. We were actually suffering for something to eat. It is still snowing. Heaviest snow I ever saw in my life. Boys are expecting a good time catching rabbits tomorrow.

Wednesday 23—The snow is from 15 to 18 inches deep. Have a beautiful day. Boys are all out catching rabbits.

Thursday 24—Heard today that we are going to No Ca under command of Maj Gen McLaws.

Friday 25—Woke up this morning & found it snowing again. No news in camp.

Saturday 26—Everything is very quiet today. Received orders this evening to cook rations & be ready to march at 7 o'clock tomorrow. Rumor says we are going to Va.

Sunday 27—Orders countermanded. Will not march until tomorrow. The snow is about all gone. It is thot that our Div will go to Gen Lee again.

Monday 28—Left camp near Greenville this morning at 7 o'clock A.M. Marched hard all day & am very tired tonight.

Tuesday 29—Woke up this morning & found it snowing. Snowed on us all day & the roads were very muddy indeed. Only marched 10 miles all day. Camped tonight at Jonesboro, Tenn.

March 1864—Wednesday 30—Took up our march again this morning. Snowed on us most of the day. Had an awful time. Had to march on the R. R. Crossed the Watauga river on the R.R. Bridge. It was very high.

Thursday 31—After a hard days march we arrived at Bristol at about 6 o'clock. Heard today that we are going to Gen Johnson.

April 1864—Friday 1—Lay in camp all day. Had a little rain.

Saturday 2—Everything is quite dull. No news. Recd a letter from Sister Em.

Sunday 3—Last night a party from our Brigade made a charge on the Post Commissary at Bristol. Lt. Wells of the 24th Geo Regt was killed, also two others badly if not mortally wounded & several others slightly. The party is now under arrest. Lt. Haddock of the 24th was in the party. It was an awful affair.

Monday 4—Went about two miles in the country today & had a most excellent dinner at the house of Mr. Hamonds.

Tuesday 5—Rained all day.

Friday 8—A day set apart by the President as a day of fasting, humiliation & prayer. Had a sermon from the Rev. Mr. Yarbrough in camp. Nothing of interest has occurred since the 5th. All quiet. It has been raining for the last week.

Sunday 10—Rained all day. *No news from home.*

Monday 11—Received orders this evening to cook rations & be ready to move at daylight.

Tuesday 12—Took the cars last night at 10 o'clock and arrived at Lynchburg. Had quite a pleasant time and plenty to eat on the way. Saw a great many ladies.

Wednesday 13—Left Lynchburg this morning at 7 o'clock on the passenger train. Had a pleasant time. Arrived at Charlotte Va about 11 o'clock A.M. & marched out one mile to camp. Saw a great *many nice* "Va" ladies.

Thursday 14—I acted commissary for the Brigade in the absence of Maj. G.

Friday 15—I visited the University of Va. Saw a great many curiosities in the Museum. Also visited the anatomical Museum. Was much pleased with the sight.

April 1864—Sunday 17—Left Charlottesville this morning on the road toward Gordonsville. Passed Montecello the residence of Thos Jefferson.

Monday 18—Arrived at or near Gordonsville Va this evening. W. D. A. came in from home.

April 1864—Friday 29—Gen Lee reviewed us today. The whole corps. Had quite a large turn out. There was also a great many prittie ladies to see us.

Saturday 30—P.L. Ardis & myself went to town (Gordonsville) today. Had a pleasant time. Saw a beautiful young ladie. Fell in love.

May 1864—Sunday 1—Wrote to Mother today. Also to Cos M—O.

Wednesday 4—Left Gordonsville at 4 o'clock P.M. Marched until 11 o'clock at night towards Fredricksburg. We lay down to rest for 3 hours.

Thursday 5—Marched hard all day. About night came upon the Yankies & drove them several miles. Camped near "Texas Va."

Friday 6—Took up our march again at 3 o'clock A.M. Marched towards Chancellorsville. Came upon the Yankies on the Plank Road at Parkers Store. They were driving Gen A. P. Hill back. We were put in immediately & drove them back after a hard fight of 3 hours. Our Brigade flanked & drove them from their works.

Saturday 7—I was on picket all night. Our whole corps was sent to the extreme right. Skirmished all day & at night was relieved by Phillips Geo Legion to rest but got orders to move. About 9 o'clock started out in the direction of Spotsylvania C. H.

Sunday 8—Marched hard all day (& last night too). Came upon the Yankies at Spotsylvania C. H. found them driving Gen Stewart back. We had a hard little fight. Drove the Yankies from the town of Spotsylvania. Oh I am so awful tired. Haven't slept any of consequence since Tuesday night. Have driven the enemy back at every point.

Monday 9—Remained behind our breastworks all day. Yankies made an attack on our lines but were repulsed at every point with great loss.

Tuesday 10—Was on picket all night. Have not slept any for the last week. Yankies charged us again but was again repulsed with heavy loss.

May 1864—Wednesday 11—Our Brigade was relieved today by Gen Kershaw & sent to support Gen Field's Div.

Thursday 12—We were aroused at daylight & ordered double quick to the right as the Yankies charged & took the works from Gen Ewel's corps. Charged and drove them back. Had an awful time. Maj

Conyers of Cobb's Legion was killed. Had 12 in my Co wounded. The Yankies had an enfilading fire on us all day. Hardest fight I ever saw or experienced.

Friday 13—Was on picket all night. Had an awful time. Rained on us. Both sides kept up heavy fire all night long. We were relieved again today & sent to the rear to rest.

Saturday 14—Had a good night's rest. No news. Yankies fell back in our front. Our Batt was sent out in front. Came on the Yankies & had a hard skirmish. No loss on our side. Returned to our lines again to rest.

Sunday 15—Rained last night on us. Our Bat was sent out again in front to feel the enemy. Drove them about two miles. Captured a great many prisoners & some 12 or 15 caissons. About night was ordered to withdraw to our lines.

Monday 16—Rec'd orders to march last night at 12 o'clock. Marched toward Gunneals Station, about 4 miles. Found the road awful muddy. Halted about daylight & camped. Wrote to Mother.

Tuesday 17—Went to wagon to change clothes. Had a long walk.

Wednesday 18—Yankies made an attack on our left before sun rise. We were ordered to the left to support Gen Wilcox Div. Was under a heavy shelling all day. Returned to our old camp at night.

Thursday 19—Remained in camp all day. All quiet in front.

Friday 20—Received orders last night to march West about 4 miles to the west of our lines to support Gen Ewel's Corps.

Saturday 21—Lay in line of battle all day. At night returned to our position on the right.

Sunday 22—Took up our march last night at dark. Marched all night towards Gunneals Station. Halted at day light. Rested an hour. The day was awful hot & dusty & I was very tired. Arrived at South Anna river about noon.

May 1864—Monday 23—Last night I slept soundly. Took our position on the line today. Heavy skirmishing all evening.

Tuesday 24[8]—Yankies fell back from our front and moved in the direction of the White House. We moved on down the river. Had a heavy Cavalry on our front on the Pamunkey River. No ration all day.

Tuesday 24—Was in front all day. Yankies drove Gen Kershaw's Brigade from the ridge. Artillery firing was kept up all day.

Wednesday 25—I was on picket all night. Had an awful time. Rained all night. Was relieved this morning & sent to the rear to rest. Received five letters, one from Cos Mollie, one from Cos Lila Mays, one from Aunt Narcissa, two from Sister Em.

---

[8] Two entries with this date.

Thursday 26—Was sent out in front again today. Yankies shelled us prettie furiously with mortars.

Friday 27—Was on picket last night. Rained on us again. Yankies advanced on us but we drove them back. Was relieved today.

Saturday 28—Yankies fell back on our front going towards the White House. We moved on down on the Pamunkey River. Had a heavy Cavalry skirmish in our front. No rations.

Sunday 29—Rested all day. Had a sermon from Rev. Mr. Pryor. Visited the 7th Geo Regt. Wrote home.

Monday 30—I was quite sick last night. Moved on the line today. Had quite a heavy skirmish just at dark. Heard good news form Gen Johnson.

Tuesday 31—Was in front all day. Sharp shooting.

June 1864—Wednesday 1—Last night moved to the right. Marched all night. Had an awful time. At 10 o'clock took our position on the front line. Advanced to feel the enemy. Had quite a hot skirmish. Drove the Yankies back. I received a slight wound in the head. It was very painful. Went to the rear till morning.

Thursday 2—Staid last night at the hospital. Rejoined my Co today. My head is yet quite sore.

Friday 3—The Yankies attacked us today in heavy force but were repulsed with great loss. Our side the loss was light.

June 1864—Saturday 4—Heavy skirmishing all day. Yankies made another charge on our works after dark. Drove them back.

Sunday 5—Heavy skirmishing all day.

Monday 6—No news. Wrote to Sister Emma.

Tuesday 7—Was on picket all night. Yankies sent in a flag of truce asking permission to bury their dead.

Wednesday 8—Was relieved today.

Thursday 9—Was sent on picket again today. Wrote to Bud.

Monday 13—This morning the enemy left our front. We followed them several miles. Took many prisoners who said the army was going to Harrison's Landing. We followed on to Frasier's Farm.

Tuesday 14—Frasier's Farm. Yankies fell back in our front.

Wednesday 15—Yankies are reported massing to the south side of Harrison's Landing.

Thursday 16—Took up our march toward Richmond. Stopped near Duns Bluff. It was awful hot.

Friday 17—Lay on the road side all day. At night crossed river at Dun's Bluff and marched toward Petersburg.

Saturday 18—Arrived at P— at 7 1/2 o'clock. things looked quite equally. Took position on the line.

Sunday 19—Our Brigade was detached to support the ... (illeg.) Army.

Monday 20—Lay in reserve all day. No news.

Tuesday 21—No change since 20th.

Wednesday 22—Gen A. P. Hill flanked and drove the Yankies from their works, capturing 4 cannon & 1600 prisoners.

Thursday 23—All quiet in front today.

June 1864—Friday 24—Was quite unwell all day.

Saturday 25—Was quite sick. Went to field hospital in the evening.

July 1864—Sunday 3—Duff　Rice was wounded night　before last while asleep in camp & died this morning at 3 o'clock. Was buried today. I wrote to his Ma.

Monday 4—It is rumored that the Yankies are moving back to the north side again.

Friday 8—Heard today of Gen Johnston's fall back to the Chattahoochee river & shelling at Turner's Ferry. My home is gone up I suppose.

July 25—We are camped at Fort Harrison. Capt King, Lt Ardis & myself visited our Gun Boats. Went aboard the "Virginia" and "Richmond". We were all pleased at the sights and curiosities.

Thursday 28—Had a skirmish near Frasier's Farm. Drove the Yankies & at night fell back.

Friday 29—Had a skirmish today near Malvern Hill. Drove the Yanks about one mile.

Saturday 30—Was on picket all night. Advanced again this morning & drove the enemy upwards of two miles to their Gun Boats at Deep Bottom. Had one man killed, several wounded. Col Hutchins was very badly wounded by a shot from the Yankie Gun Boats was very sorry to hear. He will be greatly missed by the Bat.

Sunday 31—Marched hard all night & part of today & I arrived at camp five miles from Petersburg. Heard of the explosion of Grant's mine.

August 1864—Saturday 6—Left camp today for Chesterfield Station. Don't know where we are bound for.

Sunday 7—Took cars this morning for Richmond & arrived at R— about 8 o'clock. Left immediately for Gordonsville. I was quite unwell.

Monday 8—Arrived at Gordonsville at daylight. I was unable to go farther. Was sent to the hospital.

Sunday 14—I have been quite sick since Monday last with fever. Was today transferred to Richmond. Was sent to Gen. Hospital No 4. Saw Col H.

August 1864—Monday 15—Have been quite sick all day. Was put in same ward with Lt Lidell of 16th Geo Reg.

Tuesday 16—I am much better today. Went down in the City & wrote a letter to Sister Sallie.

Thursday 18—Will leave for my command today.

Friday 19—Left Richmond yesterday & arrived at Stanton last night. Took breakfast at the American Hotel. Left Stanton this morning. Passed through Mt Sidney & put up tonight at an old church near Mt. Crawford. Marched 19 miles & was very tired. I had eggs for supper.

Saturday 20—Marched 19 miles today. Passed through Harrisonburg (Va.). Ate dinner & draw rations at that place. Rained on us all day. Have taken Qrts tonight in an old Barn 12 miles from Harrisonburg.

Sunday 21—Marched 21 miles today. Passed through New Market, Mount Jackson & Edinburgh. Camped one mile from the latter place. Drew rations at Mount Jackson. Had them cooked at old Mr. Pence's. Saw several Young Female Gals & all saw "B" who seemed quite a gallant young fellow.

Monday 22—Marched 18 miles today. Passed through Mars Town & Strasburg. Met Gem Bryant who told me that my Co with Cos D & E had been captured. Col Styles of the 6th Geo Rgt killed. Col Whitehead of Cobb's Geo Legion & Lt McMurry was also killed. Do not know what will become of me. No Co.

Tuesday 23—Marched 18 miles today. Passed through Middle Town, New Town & Mill Town & arrived at Winchester this evening before.

Wednesday 24—Spent last night at H— Mole home. Marched only about 8 or 10 miles. Camped at Bruce Town. "No rations."

Thursday 25—Marched hard all day. Marched about 15 miles. found our Brigade wagons & command all right. With them at Charlestown Va.

Friday 26—Went to the front in 4 miles of Harper's Ferry & Joined the Batt on picket. Capt Gober came in from home.

Saturday 27—Our Division fell back. Passed through Charlestown, Smithfield, Winchester & camped near the latter place.

August 1864—Monday 29—Moved today about 4 miles towards Berryville to do picket duty.

Tuesday 30—Went to a house & got a good dinner.[9]

---

[9] The notebook/dairy ends here, although WRM finished out the war. If WRM kept another diary, it has been lost, and no one in the family knows its location.

William Rhadamanthus Montgomery

William Rhadamanthus Montgomery and
family years after the War.

William Rhadamanthus Montgomery just before 1900.

William Rhadamanthus Montgomery and
new wife Emma Northcutt.

The Letters of
William Rhadamanthus
Montgomery

Camp Palmetto near Manassas (no date - 1861. EKA)

My Dear Sister

We are encamped in the woods near Manassas Station in about 2 miles of the great Manassas Gap. We left Richmond on last Friday night & arrived at Manassas about 10 o'clock Saturday night. When we arrived we found our presence if not our services very much needed as it was thought that the enemy was advancing on that point.

A scouting party was sent out in the direction of Alexandria consisting of seven hundred men. They were out all night. As it was late when we arrived & no wagons to carry our tents to the place of encampment, we all spread down our blankets prepared to spend the night... (illeg.) with nothing save the broad canopy of heaven. Sister it was indeed a beautiful sight to see 2000 men all lying on the bare ground & undergoing the many hardships for the sake of his country. There is at this place about 9000 men all well drilled & armed. We have two alarms, one on Sunday morning & I am happy to say the P.G. were by no means the last on the field but among the first. We all loaded & were furnished with forty rounds of cartridges. After everything was quiet we all marched over to an old field & pitched tents Sunday as it was. I believe I worked as hard as ever I did in my life.

On Monday everything was quiet untill about ten o'clock when an alarm was given & we were all ordered to march in few minutes to where our first Regt is stationed (about 8 mi.) as it was reported it had been attacked. But when we had marched as far as this place through the dust (2000 strong 6 miles) we were met by a picket Guard who informed us the report was not so, but one of the Picket Guards had been shot. So we encamped or rather stopped at this place, & have been here ever since with not one tent untill yesterday. We all slept as we could on the ground.

I was on Picket Guard all day Tuesday & untill Wednesday morning. We have to walk nearly all day & night, sometimes five & six miles from where we are stationed. It is indeed very hard. I came very near freezing night before last as we had no tents, had to sleep out & we had a very heavy frost. We are situated on a beautiful River called Bull run, & I am now sitting on the bank writing on a rock. While sitting here dear Sister I often think of you & dear little Willie & Lizzie. Sometimes I think I would give anything in the world to see you all. I often dream of you all while sleeping out under the shade of some beautiful tree. We are all employed in raising a breast work. I know it would make you laugh to see Bill A. shoveling dirt & throwing the pick. I assure you it goes prettie hard with him. We are now in a days march to Washington City about 1200 miles from home the way we came. Gen Lee has come and says we will all sleep in Alexandria in a few nights. We have arrested three spies & our com had the pleasure of catching two of them. We indeed have a beautiful place here for a battle. The banks of the River are about 15 feet high and solid rock. We are building on top of that. I received your kind note a few minutes before I left R but had not time to answer it. I had come to the conclusion that you did not care for me or had forgotten me.

I have been quite unwell for some time. I have a severe cold caught by sleeping out. I did think I was going to be really sick, *but hope I will not.* I have not had anything to eat untill yesterday for several days. As I was relieved from picket guard, Bill David & myself went about three miles for something to eat. We went to an old lady & told her for heaven sake to give us something to eat & we would pay whatever she charged. She fussed about a little & gave us some bacon, some cornbread, butter &

coffee & I tell you I never enjoyed a meal more in my life. We paid her & left for camp. Told the other boys & be assured they were but few minutes in going. Most everybody near here are Yankies or Union men & they charge very high for everything--biscuit 4 cents, very small chickens 25 cts, large 40 cts, and other things in proportion. Some of our boys went out and killed 2 sheep & a hog, but it did not last long.

Col. Kershaw said if we did not get some meat in a few days he would appoint so many men out of each com to provide meat at the expense of the people. They have pressed every wagon into service in the whole country to haul provisions but cannot get them fast enough. Bolan Glover got a box by express yesterday. His Ma said if he got that one she would send another. I wish you would see & if so make me two flannel shirts (like my coat) & send in the box. I want them for over shirts (you know what kind) & tell Mr. Haley to send 2 Pr Suspenders the best he has & any thing else if he wants to (that is to eat) & also one Pocket Glass. *Miss Lula Heaven bless her soul* sent me a beautiful silk skull cap & a small pocket containing buttons, thread, needles & pins which I found very useful. My cap is indeed a beautiful one with my name worked on it. She has proven so far to be my best friend & may in after days be my *dearest friend*, that is when I return.

If you have anything to eat that you think would satisfy the hunger of a soldier you can send it in that box with Mrs. Glover. If you send anything you must offer at least to pay part of the express. Tell Mr. Haley to write to me oftener & not wait for me to write first all the time. I have but little time & a very poor chance. Tell him if he has any thing that is good to eat to send it. You may send him this letter if you wish as he is one of my best friends. I often think of him.

Write soon & tell me how he (J.T.H.) & Miss Mary is getting on. I expect in a few days our communications will be stopped. If so I hope you all will write often, as we will be allowed to receive but not to answer. I must close. Give my kindest regards to Misses Mittie & Margaret and all the young ladies of my acquaintance you see. My love to Aunt Frank, Ben & Joe Kirkham & J.T.Haley & tell all the darkies howdy.

I hope to write you soon from Alexandria. If you do send a box, send it to Manassas Station care of Col. Kershaw 2nd Reg. So Ca Volunteers, & direct letters as before (to Richmond Va.).

I am as ever your loving Bud
William Montgomery

Tell Bud to tell H.M.Mainert (?) I will answer his letter in a few days. Would do it now but have to work. You would not know us. We all wear striped shirts while at. I have blistered my hands already & we are all very much sun burnt. Excuse all mistakes & Penmanship.

Camp Beauregard June 11, 1861

Dear Pa & Mother

I received your kind & truly interesting letter (Mothers) & I assure you I was indeed glad to hear form you all. We are well & enjoying ourselves very well indeed. Your kind letter came to just as I came off drill last night. I heard Buck was in Richmond but we are now about 200 miles from there. Our two Reg's are the foremost on the field. We are in a days march of Washington City (24 miles) & about 30 miles form Alexandria. Our 1st Reg had a fight last week. Our side killed 35 men & took 3 prisoners & about 15 horses. We were ordered to march to their assistance but when we had gone about four miles we were turned back as the fight was over. We have been expecting a fight here for several days & when we lie down at night we keep our guns loaded by our side.

I think there is enough young folks to fight the battles without old men leaving their families. So Pa I think you had better abandon the idea & stay at home. As I think your family is well represented already, as I sometimes feel I could fight a small army myself. Mother you spoke of sending me some clothes. I sent to Em for some & if she sends them I will be supplied. It is best not to have many at a time as they are very heavy to carry. As day before yesterday was Sunday & a prettie day, Bill Davis, Bill A., Payson Ardis & myself got a pass form our Capt. & went out in search of something to eat. After walking about four or five miles we came to a house & called for dinner & got what we poor soldiers call good, but you would think quite different. After dinner we thought as we had plenty of time we would all take a walk. Somehow Payson & myself got lost from the other two, & we well knew we could not pass the sentinels nor the pickets without a permit. Just imagine our feelings four or five miles from home & it nearly night & we without our pass.

We wandered about untill we found an old house, went in & made ourselves at home. We laid down on the floor, put our coats under our heads & soon forgot all & fell a sleep & slept soundly. Next morning we slipped round & got to Gen Beauregards head quarters & got a permit from him that brought us home, where we found our Capt quite uneasy about us. I have been very sick since I wrote you last but am better. I was on guard all night Friday night & all day Saturday. It rained very hard most all the time & I was afraid I would be sick but was not. Col Gartrells Reg passed through Manassas Saturday. Bolan Glover & Payson went up & saw them but I was on guard I could not go.

Mother you did not tell me what company the Wood boys went with. I hope you & *Pa* will write often & tell me all the news in general & tell Sibe to write to me. All in camp seem to enjoy themselves very much indeed. Some are cooking, some dancing, some eating & some playing the violin. We are in a beautiful country. We are in plain view of the Blue ridge & Allegheny mountains & we are in about 10 or 12 miles of Mt. Vernon. Oh! I am so hungry for something good to eat & I would give most anything some little "Nick Nacks" to eat, as I was so used to them at home. I have just come from Battalion drill. Oh! I would be so glad to meet up with Buck out here & I do hope he will be sent here. It is thought this will be the great battle field. We have about 10,000 to 12,000 men here now & they are still coming. We have such a nice company & such kind officers, but we have very poor fare indeed. Sometimes we have coffee & sea biscuit & not one thing else & the coffee without sugar. I bought 2 lbs sugar the other day & paid 25 cts per pound (50 for 2 lbs). The way the people impose us poor soldiers is indeed a sin. I hope you will look over all mistakes & excuse bad writing as I am sitting down on the ground & using my knee as a desk. P̲a̲ I hope you will abandon the idea of leaving your family as Buck & myself will do enough for us all & there is time enough yet & besides camp life will not agree with you.

The whole country about here is almost entirely abolition & some of the grandest scoundrels you ever heard of. One of Brooks Guards was coming out of his tent the other day & another was just going in with his gun when it went off & whole load passed through the tope of his head, the one coming out, killing him instantly. It was indeed a sad sight. My love to all & write soon. Kiss Charlie. Bill Anderson & all the Geo boys all join me in love to you all. As ever your most obt [=obedient] son.

W. R. Montgomery

Excuse pencil I have no ink. I am in great haste.

Bull Run
Camp Beauregard
June 20th 1861
(9 o'clock at night)

Dear Bro'
Your highly prized & truly interesting favor has just been read. I was really glad to hear you were all well. We are all packed up now and waiting for orders to march. We will leave in a few minutes for Fairfax (14 miles) as we learned five thousand men were in a few miles of that place & it is thought will attack the place before day. We will march about six thousand to that place tonight & if they (the 5,000 Federal troops) do not attack us by day light we will march on them & drive them back. We are all well & in high spirits and anxious to get off although you know 14 miles is no small distance. Col Gregg had a little brush Monday. He killed, wounded & took prisoners 200.

The way he managed to successfully was he was expecting the enemy on the cars & took 24 men & their cannon & placed them in six hundred yards of R.R. & as the cars passed he fired into them & such another jumping over board you have never heard of. Col Gregg only fired 24 guns. The cars began to retreat & ran off & killed some by that. *So you see we raked in a few of them.* There was on board 800 men, (quite a nice fight 800 to 24) & they did not even fire one gun on Col Gregg but took to their heels & went it double quick. Oh! dear Bro you can not imagine my feeling when I read the probability of you visiting Manassas. I would give any thing on earth to see you & I do hope you will come. I will agree to refund your expenses if you will only come, business or no business. *Oh! do come.* Give my kindest love to Miss Lula when you see her & you may also tell her that 'ere you read this I will in all probability be engaged with the enemy & for all I know I may be numbered with the slain, but hope I may be spared to see her once more. Oh I do hope I will see you in a short time & if you come you must bring me something to eat (nice). We have a few rations of bacon & some hard biscuit to last us five days as we expect to be gone that long. Dear Bro' you will please excuse all mistakes & writing as I am in such a hurry to get off I hardly know what I am writing. Oh I would give the world to see Sister Em, Lizzie, Willie, Miss Lula & yourself. You really do not know how I appreciate your kind letters. It really seems you, Em & Miss Lula are all that care for me. Dear Bro I cannot help but tell you what kind officers we have. I really did not know that an officer could be so kind. They are always telling us what pleasure they take in accommodating us & it seems we Georgians are the favorites with them. *They are so very kind.*

I wish I could see you & Miss Lula acting on the stage. I knew I would commit a sin loving her (Miss Lou). I hope you will see her often & kindly remember me to her, & thank her many times for those nice eatables she sent me. Jim Kilby has acted just as I expected. One would have thought when I left there that he would be off to war in a few days. I would write you more but I am afraid the call will come before I close.

Everything in camp is very quiet, & I expect you have more excitement in Atlanta in one day than we have here in one week. We are now at a post of honor as well as one of great danger. I do hope you write often as you have no idea how much I appreciate your kind letters. All the Boys are anxious to see you & all look upon you as our best friend. Payson Ardis & myself are just like Bros. We are always together. We have at this place (or near here) 25,000 men ready to march. We would make a nice show in Washington City. I must close as the drum has just finished beating for us all to fall in & I must go. Hoping to see you or hear form you soon I am as ever your loving Bro. My love to all.

W. R. Montgomery

When I write again I will try to give you some news, as I am in too much of a hurry at present.

I will write you again as soon as I can get a chance.

All boys send love to you. I think it quite doubtful about drawing on you as we are 200 miles Richmond & you know that is the nearest point you can draw on. I will do what I can as I need some very bad indeed.

Near Frederick Md.
Sept. 8th 1862

My Dear Sister
    As Lt McCleskey leaves here to morrow for old Geo, I thought I would write you a few lines to let you know of my where-abouts. I caught up with Legion last Friday night at Leesburg. Next morning we all crossed the Potomac. It was indeed a beautiful sight to see our brave soldiers wading the river (which was about 1/2 mile wide). We have suffered a great deal for something to eat. Payson & I had a hard time in catching our Regt. Came as far as Rapidan on the cars & as the bridge was burnt by the Yankees we had to wade. We then marched on by Culpepper to Leesburg, a distance of about 95 miles. Had nothing to eat but corn which we took from the fields on the road side. Camped out every night. Passed by Warranton Springs (White Sulphur). It was the most beautiful place I ever saw. The Y's burnt down one of the principal buildings & in fact the whole county is laid in waste. We now have possession of the B & O R.R. & today have been blowing up the Bridge across the Manoxy River. It is about 2 miles to Frederick City which is about the size of Atlanta. Oh my dear Sister this is truly one of the prettiest countries I ever saw. We made a force march to get here. *Had not had anything to eat in two days.* I went to a house to buy something & met two of the nicest young ladies (except one) you ever saw. They gave me some nice cornbread & a saucer of the nicest Raspberry jelly you ever saw. Said Oh they were so glad to see us.
    Tell Mother where I am, also that I am well. Can't write as we have no mail.
    I did not get a hand in the last fight. Was mighty sorry but it may be all for the best. The L- lost several men but did not fire a gun. Every thing is quite cheap here. Bacon

(nice ham) is selling at from 10 to 12 cts, chickens at 10 cts, butter 10 cts, molasses 75 cts, lard 10 cts, nice shoes $2.00 & in fact everything is very cheap.

My regard to Miss Lou & tell her I will write the first opportunity. Haven't had a letter in 3 weeks. We are now lying in an old clover field. Have nothing to write on but my knee. It is just 40 miles to Baltimore & about 12 miles from the Penn line. Boys are all well. give my love to Bro "Chal" & tell him to write soon. Gen Lee's head qrtrs are Fredrick. My love to Aunt Fran, Eliza, Mittie, & Mag. I am your loving Bro in haste.

W

We are all very tired. Spent yesterday in cooking up 3 days rations.

Sister Em, please excuse writing. Coffee is worth 29 cts & sugar 20 & 12.

Kiss Lillie & Willie

I lost many friends in the fight.

Camp near Winchester
  Oct. 4th 1862

My Dear Bro Chal,

I learned through Mr. Ruede yesterday who left Marietta some ten days ago that you was *quite sick* but that you was some better than you had been. I was indeed sorry to hear such news & do hope you are almost well again. I have been quite uneasy about you all for some time past as I haven't heard from any of you since Lemon came on. Hope I will hear in a few days. We are still lying here drilling a little. My dear Sister I must stop rite here to read your letter of the 24th which was just handed me a minute ago.

You don't know how glad I am to hear that Chal is improving. Hope to see him soon. Oh! How glad I would be to see him out *here.* Wish you Lizzie & Willie could come with him. *Oh!* I was so glad to receive your letter today. Mr. Ruede will leave for Georgia next Monday. Will send this by him. It is reported, and believed by some in camp that Gen Longstreet's Corps will be sent to So Ca & Georgia. Hope it is true. I then might stand a chance to get home a short while. tell Chal I was indeed sorry my boots didn't fit. They were large enough every other way, only too low in the instep. I sold them to Maj. James Waddell of the 20th Geo. Suppose you heard that John Waddell was killed in Maryland.

You asked me how I like Maryland & how I enjoyed myself. Well it is the prettiest country I ever saw, but as for enjoyment I don't want to go any more & I think we had better let (Md) alone for she seems joined to her *Idols* "(Union)".

I am now Orderly Sergeant of Camp "L". Have a good deal to do but no more standing post in the rain & cold & besides I get nearly twice the pay of a private ($21.

per month). Be sure & send me on first chance a nice Pocket Blank Book for a roll book. Payson & Cos Sam are quite well & look finely. Bill A- is about as usual(not well & Not rite sick & very low spirited). I am well pleased with Dr. Gober & F. Lowry as Officers. We are all in a mess together. Have a good time together.

I wrote you a few days ago by Mr. Hardridge. Haven't heard from Mother since I left Richmond.

Has Col Boyd been assigned to a post? He told me in R- that he had applied for one. Heard from some of the Boys that you had a revival in Marietta. Was glad to hear it for if a country ever did need the prayers of a People I think we need them at this particular time. Tell me who all joined the church. I am now in the worst fix for clothing I have ever been since the war. Have but one old calico shirt to my name & one old worn out pr drawers & nearly barefooted. Our Co drew 3 pair of shoes today but we had 4 men entirely barefooted so as I had some old ones I could not get any. Oct. 5 - Last night we moved camp to a little village called Boontown. Had a rainy, windy night & also quite cold. Oh! how I would like to see you all. Tell Chal to be sure & come to see me if he does come out here. Give my love to Aunt Frank & family, also to all friends, Miss Lou not excepted.

Tell Lizzie & Willie I hope to see them this winter if we get to the coast. Dr. Gober says he will do all he can to get me a furlough. Nothing more at present. Write soon to your loving

"Brum"

Excuse all mistakes

Bro Chal—please excuse this letter as when commenced it to you, but soon after I find it is to Sister Em. Am in such a hurry I know not what to do. WRM

Camp near Fredricksburg Va
Dec. 7th 1862

My dear Mother,

Tis indeed with much pleasure I take my seat to write you a few hurried lines to inform you that I am quite well & progressing finely in the capacity of a soldier. Today is quite cold indeed, the ground is covered several inches in snow & I am sorry to say many, yes many, of our brave soldiers are but illy prepared for it. A great many that I know of are entirely barefooted & but very few have over one blanket & you know that one blanket to the man & he exposed to the pelting snow without any tent or shelter of any kind, save what he can readily construct of brush is not enough. This morning as went to the branch to wash I had to brake the ice & before I could get to the fire my hair & whiskers was a solid mat of ice. We have a hard time for duty, have to go on Picket in the town every day or two & remain for two days at a time. it would not be so bad only we have to go & come on Picket after night so as to keep the Yankies from knowing that we are in town as they would shell the place if they knew a body of troops were in the city. We go in at night & send the men out on the bank of the river on Post (& they will not fire on a single man). Just one the other side of a high hill the Yankies have a great many *large* guns bearing on the city ready to open on us at any moment.

Their Pickets & ours are in plain view in short musket range, but both sides have orders not to fire. I had an offer to go over under a flag of truce day before to carry over some ladies, but another sergt in our company wanted to go & also he was a better oarsman than myself so I gave up for him to go in my place. I sent over some later Richmond papers & they readily gave in exchange the New Herald, Bal Sun & in fact all of the latest Northern papers. Got old Abe's message. They had many questions to ask about the War. Why is you, Pa   or Henry one or some of you don't write. I haven't had but one letter from you since I was in R- in the summer & that was the one sent by Maj Griffis & I did not get it until over a month after it was written. I know Henry could write if he would & as for you & Pa you are in part excusable for I know old folks have something else to think about beside writing letters.

I heard the other day that Sister Em had gone down to stay with you for the winter. Oh I am so sorry for her & her dear little ones. Oh that I could but return home & provide & care for them for Bro C was indeed to me a kind friend & a loving Bro & I shall ever love his *dear dear* children. I wrote to Sister Em a few days ago but directed the letter to Marietta. heard that Capt J.M.Johnson would leave for Va on the 5th inst. Hope he will bring me a pair of pants & coat as I am very much in need of them. If you did not send by him please send by Jos T. Lowrey who will leave about the 1st of Jan. 1863 & any thing else you want to send me. Send Henry too if you will & let him see how we have to fare. Tell him to put on soldier clothes & he can get (in Atlanta) transportation free & as for going back he can get back for $15.00 & I will pay that readily to see him. Let him come with Joe L-

Hope we will be going back to the coast soon anyway & he can go back with us for nothing. Cos Sam, Payson & Bill A. says tell Col Ozburn (Pa) to send a bottle of "*good old corn.*" It can't be had here. I saw some sell at $1.50cts per drink the other night & very small ones at that. I got to eat supper at a table the other night in town at an old free Negroes house. Had sausage. Had to pay $1.50cts for it.

(Bottom of page; no closing or signing.)

Camp near Fredricksburg, VA
December 17th 62

My Dear Aunt Frank

Doubtless you will be somewhat surprised to receive a letter from me at this late date, but dear Aunt Frank I have often wished for a correspondence with some one of the family but when dear sister was in Marietta I could hear from you all through her & I thought it useless to be so formal as to keep or rather ask a correspondence with you when I could hear so often.

Since Sister Em has left Marietta I took occasion to write to Miss Eliza but she very much unlike myself has never taken the occasion to answer me, either the one way or the other. I did not think she would treat her *cousin* that way. I think she might have given me some kind of an answer, but it may be she has written & I have never received it, for I really do think she would have given me an acceptance or a refusal to my request. But I will wait to see if I may yet hear from her. Hope I may.

And now Aunt Frank as I have no one to keep me posted as regards the news about the City of Marietta I hope you will be at your leisure from time to time give me few lines concerning the affairs in general in that section of the country. I suppose you have heard before this of our big battle in which our Legion took a conspicuous part, but I will try to give a few of the leading particulars which may be of some little interest to you. The Yankies occupy one side of the river & we the other & the city of Fredricksburg is right on our bank of the river, & our pickets stand on the bank in the edge of the city. On last Thursday night the Yankies drove in our pickets, put down their pontoon bridges & began to cross. Our forces fell back through town & gave up the place. All day Friday they were crossing, & Aunt Frank it would have made your blood run cold to have seen their great numbers coming over to oppose our little handful of brave soldiers. They were making ready all day Friday for one grand demonstration on Saturday. Saturday about 11 o'clock they began their advance & our brave & beloved Gen Cobb placed his Brigade behind a stone fence & pulled off his hat & waving it over his head exclaimed, "Get ready Boys here they come" & they did come *sure*.

We waited until they got within about 200 yards of us & rose to our feet & poured volley after volley into their ranks which told a most deadening effect. They soon began to waver & at last broke from the *rear*, but the shouts of our brave soldiers had scarcely died away when we saw coming another column more powerful & seemingly more determined than the first (if possible) but only a few rounds form our brave & well tried men was necessary to tell them that they had undertaken a work a little too hard. But before they had entirely left the field another column & another & still another came to their support. But our well aimed shots were more than they could stand so about night they were compelled to give up the field covered with their dead.

The whole time of the engagement our brave & gallant Gen Cobb was encouraging on his men untill a shot form the enemy's cannon gave him his mortal wound. He was on the right of our Co, only a few feet from me when wounded. Payson Ardis being one of our litter bearers ran to him & I never shall forget his last look as they laid him on the litter to bear him from the field. His last words to his men were, "I am only wounded Boys, hold your ground like brave men."

It was to our cause a most brilliant victory but I regret to say Geo. lost one of her brightest jewels, a noble Statesman & a brave & gallant Gen & as such we greatly deplore his loss.

Our beloved Col Cook was killed before the engagement was fairly commenced. His presence in camp as an officer as well as an associate is greatly missed, for he was loved by all. Capt. Johnson who had only been with us a few hours, being Sen Officer had to take command of the Legion but he had only gone a few steps untill he was wounded in the foot. Lt. Peak was then ordered to act as Maj but he had hardly taken command when he was wounded (badly) in the throat. Our line of battle was about 8 to 10 miles long & the fight was genrl along the whole line. In front of where our Legion fought was buried over 1100 Yankies besides what was carried off; also the wounded. I have been in many engagements before, but I never saw in my life such a slaughter. Our loss was only 14 killed 59 wounded in the Legion. Bill Tenant was one of the killed. Our Co only lost one killed & one wounded. We drove the Yankies back across the river & our pickets were now holding their same old posts. I saw a Yankie paper since the battle. They acknowledge a loss of from 18,000 to 20,000 & a complete shipping. During the fight our legion got out of ammunition & I thought we would have to come to charge bayonets on they, but just in the "nick" of time here came the old 2nd S.C.Vols. like so many wild Indians. I tell you I felt good, for we had shot away 70 rounds of cartridge & the Yankies were still coming. The once beautiful city of Fredricksburg is almost in ruins. There hardly a house that is not torn to pieces by shall & shot from cannon & a great many burnt to ashes.

Tell Misses Mittie, Margaret & Elisa they might take it upon themselves to write to a *poor cousin* in the Army. If so I will most heartily appreciate it & will promptly answer to the best of my ability. Aunt Frank if you have time & feel so disposed will you let me hear from you soon. Tell Miss Eliza I am still waiting for my answer, still hoping some good breeze will at last bring it, for you

know it is an ill wind that blows no one good. My love to
Mr. K & all the family. Hoping to hear from you soon I
am in haste

Your Loving Nephew
W. R. Montgomery

Please excuse writing & all mistakes

———————

Camp McLaws Near Fredricksburg, Va.
April 1863

My Dear Aunt Frank
T's indeed with much pleasure I now seat myself to
drop you a few hurried lines from which you will learn
that I am quite well & some times in good spirits, but
some times since my arrival in camp I have been rather
home sick.

Aunt Frank I would have written to you before now
but I have had so much to do & again I felt so little like
writing that I have put off writing untill now. I hope you
will excuse my letter today as I feel not at all like writing,
but I have put off so long now I fear you have thought
already that I have forgotten you.

I received a letter from Miss Eliza the other day. Was a
little surprised when I saw a letter for me postmarked
Stilesboro, Geo., but when I opened it I thought then I
might have known better for I might have known that she
(Miss Eliza) could not long remain from Stilesboro, for
well do I know that place has a great attraction for her.
Tell her when you next write her that she certainly does
love her Uncle John very much. Aunt Frank I have no news
to tell you that will interest you. We can see plainly from
our camp the Yankie Balloons. There was three or four up

all day yesterday & from their manoeuvres I think it very evident that some grand move is in anticipation.

We received orders the other night to cook rations & be ready to move at a moments notice. I thought the time had again arrived when would commence our long & tiresome marches, but as good luck would have it for once we did not have to leave. But I am looking everyday for orders to leave, & when we begin our marches Heaven only knows when & where we will stop. We have just heard a few minutes ago that Gen Longstreet was killed in a skirmish yesterday. Am indeed sorry to hear it & do not want to believe it, for he is one of our gallant officers & one who knows but few equals & no superiors. The Yankies say that we have a new Gen in command of our army & say his name is *General Starvation* & I think for once they are about right, for we only get 4 ounces of bacon & one small pound of flour & sometimes a little salt. We generally draw rations for three days at a time & eat them up in two & do without until we draw again. I received a letter from Bud day before yesterday. He was quite well & in good spirits. Had a small fight with the Yankie Gun Boats on the Tennessee River. He is at or near Tuscumbia, Ala. I also heard from Mr. J.T. Haley. He was well & at Shelbyville, Tenn. He participated very extensively in the great Battle of Murfresboro & came out all safe.

Aunt Frank I forgot to tell you Miss Lou has given me the *"mitten"* at last. I suppose she prefers Captain William to myself. You must keep this a secret & tell it to no one. I suppose people will have so much to talk about now, or it may be that they are about out of talkable matter & will seize upon this & discuss its causes & effects. So if you happen to hear anything on the subject I will expect you to reveal it to me. I will tell you more about it some other time. How is Miss Mittie getting on with her school & also Miss Maggie with her studies (Geography of the Heavens &c).

I can distinctly hear now while I am writing a very heavy cannonading above us on the river. Suppose they are having a little fight up that way all to themselves. Well if they don't think enough of us to ask us up to help them they may fight alone. *I don't care much about fighting any way, would you* Tell Miss Maggie I had such a nice time with Mr. Sam Weems last Sunday. I know you will laugh at the idea of me having a nice time with a man, but why not. We have no lady associates so we must make the best of our male associates. I believe I am about to fall out with the fair sex generally. I mean the unmarried ones or they with me I cannot say which. I wrote Walter a few lines some ten days ago, but have heard through Sister Em that he & Mr. Kirkham had gone to Florida (the land of flowers). Aunt Frank will beg of you to excuse all mistakes & bad writing as the boys are all talking to me about my sweet [heart, drawn in letter] & to cap all, I was out playing with Cos Sam this morning as children generally do & playing the *fool* generally knocked the bark off my hand about the size of a piece of chalk. My love to all, & write soon to Your Loving Nephew
    in haste
    W.R.Montgomery

Ask Miss Margaret how Little Nat is getting on & when is he going to leave for the Army. I presume she is having a very good time, while he is at home. Also ask her how is my *little* Cousin Carrie.

Tell *Miss Moon* if you see her *Mr. Moon* is quite well. I must stop my nonsense & bring my letter to a focus. My love all & kiss Miss Maggie again for me. WRM

Cos Sam or Capt. Harris rather sends love to you & says "*tell her you please*".

Sunday the 19th. I will send my watch to Mr. Ruede. Wish you would send & get it, & give it to Sister Em. I got up & called the Roll. My hand is quite sore this morning.

We have to go on inspection in a few minutes. Sunday is a big day in the Army. Wish I could be in old Marietta today. Think I would go to church.

Please excuse all mistakes as I find from reading they are not a few. The boys all keep up such a talking & you know I must hear what they say, hence so many mistakes.

On the Bank of the Rappahannock (Banksford)
Thursday May 7th 63

My Dear Mother & Sister

I wrote you a few lines yesterday to let you know that I was yet safe & Oh! have I not indeed been fortunate? & ought I not be thankful? I think so but I fear not enough.

We left our old camp yesterday one week ago for Fredricksburg. The Yankies had crossed over in great force. We immediately took position in our trenches & held them in check untill Thursday evening. We learned from scouts that their main Army had crossed some miles above & was then marching in our rear & that the army in our front was only trying to draw our attention untill those in our rear could come up. Or if we attempted to leave, those in our front would take possession of our works.

But you must recollect our gallant Gen Lee is always wide awake. So Thursday night after dark Gen Lee scattered Gen Early's Division along our entire front & took the remainder of his army & set out to meet Gen Hooker & his Grand Army. Marched all night. Came upon the Yanks Friday. Drove them before us like sheep until Saturday they made a stand. Our Division (Gen McLaw's) held them in front untill old "Stone Wall" & Gen A.P.Hill would go round & take them in the rear, which they accomplished very nicely.

I forgot to tell you about the Sharp Shooters. Gen Wofford had 50 men detailed from each Regt in the Brigade (5) to form a battalion of Sharp Shooters. Bill Anderson is recommended to the President for Capt, myself for *first Lieut* & two others for 2nd & 3rd Lts.

We are in camp to ourselves & are known as the 1st Geo "sharpshooters" but have no commissions yet. Payson Ardis is recommended as 1st Lt in the Co next to ours (the Co from the 16th Geo). I tell you our little Battalion won quite a name in the 6 days fight. Perhaps you don't know what our duty is. Well, I will tell you. We are always in front of the Brigade, about 300 to 400 yds., to clear out the way & I tell you we done it too, to perfection. You ought to hear Gen Wofford praise us. Saturday evening our little Battalion charged the Yankies breast work, one whole Brigade behind it, charged three times but the fire was hot from the enemy. We had to fall back. Our loss was quite heavy. Soon Sunday morning the Gen sent us in again. We charged again under the most deadly fire. Got within a few feet of the works, but it was fixed with brush that we could not climb then & had to fall back. Our loss was again more.

Lost our Col Patten. P.Ardis Co lost Capt & 2nd Lt (not killed but badly wounded) (also 8 men). Our Co lost 2nd Lt & one man killed dead & 8 badly wounded. Other companies lost in proportion. Our 3rd Lt was also wounded. Only Bill & myself in command of our Co & I am acting commissary for the Batt in the bargain, & if we do not fail to get our commissions & everything works out well I will get the position of commissary (Rand of Capt) - hope we will not fail. Old Gen Wofford sent up great recommendation to old Jeff. But I must finish about the battles. When we fell back Sunday morning we only fell back under a hill only a few yards. About 12 o'clock Gen Jackson began to drive them in & set them to mining so we thought it a good time to charge again. So at them we went like so many wild Indians. Fired only two or three rounds when they showed a white flag. We all rushed forward & found that about 800 or 900 men had surrendered to only a small Batt of "Sharp Shooters" (one whole Reg 27th Connecticut & many more). We sent them to the rear & pushed forward. Met Gen "Stone Wall's" Corps & soon had Gen Hooker & his Grand Army in full rout. Gens McLaws & Anderson left Gen Jackson to pursue them, & brought their Divisions back towards Fredricksburg to meet Yankies that crossed over at that place, who had succeeded in forcing Gen Early Division back & capturing our hights around the city. Our Division (Gen McLaws) (11,000 men) took position in their front & held them in check while Gens Early & Anderson marched round & took them in rear & on their flank which took till late Monday evening. At the signal forward we all moved at once. The Yankies fought well at first but when they found we were on three sides of them they made tracks for the river.

We still moved forward, pressing them at every point untill 1 o'clock at night, capturing many prisoners. Sharp Shooters made a charge in a pine thicket, not knowing anybody was in it, dark as Egypt, fired a volley & you ought to have heard the Yanks beg for quarter. Took a Lt Col & about half a Reg.

We pushed forward as far as we thought prudent in the night. Layed down on the road side to sleep, but had not been asleep long when the Yankie cavalry made a dash upon us & caused quite an excitement. Shot all among us before we could get up, but we soon put them to flight.

I was quite unwell all during the fights but hated to give up. Had a hard chill one night & very high fever & I assure I was almost tired to death when the Yankies surrendered. Oh! I was so sorry that poor Willie Ruede was killed. He was such a nice fellow, was my particular friend. Bill & I intended giving him Ordly Sergt of our Co provided it did not burst up. (*Hope it may hold good*). If nothing prevents we will have one of the nicest little commands in the army. Hope *old Jeff* will send our commissions.

You must excuse writing today as it has been raining for two or three days & we have been lying here on the river bank without tents. I am now sitting under my blanket to keep dry. If Henry comes out please send me a pair of pants, also my hat, as I much in need of them.

We are burying the Yankies today & have been for several days, not done yet. Their loss was very heavy. We took about 10,000 prisoners. Some think the enemy is not less than 25,000 to 30,000. I took a good many trophies but was so sick & tired had to throw them away. Have several Ambrotypes yet. Will send them if get a chance. Got plenty of *good coffee* & sugar.

My love to all & kiss the little ones often for me. Bless them how I do want to see them all. Kiss little Baby many times for me. I am in hast. Your loving Son & Bro.

W. R. Montgomery
Don't consider me Lt yet, only Sergt.

Camp near Culpepper (Tent) "Flora Temple"
June 11th, 1863

My Dear Sister Em

Your dear welcome missive bearing date of June 3rd
has just been received & I assure you dear Sister I was
indeed glad to hear from you, for it really does seem to
me sometimes that you all have forgotten me & that I
have but few friends. Just imagine my surprise when I
saw Henry yesterday come marching up when thought he
was at home. I started him off for home about a week
ago, do not recollect what day nor do I know now what
today is if it was to save me, I only heard some one say it
was the 11th of June. Well Henry got as far as R- & met
up with Mr. Donalson our Legion Sutter (who was quite a
friend of Bro Chal's, also a very warm friend of Uncle Jas
Young). Mr. Donalson it seems took quite a fancy to
Henry & begged him to stay with him as clerk & as you
see he consented so to do.

He is to give him $25 per month & board. He will or at
least ought to have a good time, always have a waggon to
ride & sleep in.

Henry I find is quite a wild chap to his age, but he
makes many friends where're goes. He is not afraid to
hold up his head. I really believe he knows as many or
more men now than I do. They all like him very much &
think him quite smart & by the way he is a right fast Boy.

I wrote you a few days ago. Hope you have rec'd it
before now.

We lay in the woods some two days after I wrote you.
Our Cavalry got into a fight in which they were cut up
badly & driven back. Our Corps (Gens Hood & McLaws
Divisions) were ordered down to reinforce. Thought we
would have a big fight but the Yankies took the hint &
recrossed the river.

Our Cavalry under Gen Stewart numbers about from 15,000 to 20,000. Our Batt of Sharp Shooters has been called out again & I think this time will permanently organize & I will be first Lieut, Newt Gober will be Capt. We are now in camp to ourselves. Think all will be well, hope so at least. Don't think I will get commissary as we have a new Col, as you know Col Patton was killed, but am very well satisfied with my position.

You must not consider me Lt yet, not untill I get my commission (*but address me the same*). I am very much pleased with Lt. Gober for my Capt as he is one of my best & most intimate friends. Henry, Dr. Gober & myself have just finished dinner. We all eat out of a frying pan. Had fried meat & bread. I think we will leave here soon, but where to I know not. Some seem to think the next battle will be on the plains of Manassas & that not far distant. I think it does seem that enough lives have already been lost on one field.

You spoke about Miss Lou Boyd. Your opinion and mine about her is the same. I know she is good, kind & even all I could ask her to be. I know she is not prettie nor smart but as you say, I think she has a true loving heart, but dear Sister I saw a good excuse to break off our correspondence & I took advantage of it before things might go too far. I know I have gone too far already, but could not help, for sometimes I think, yes I know I *love* her, but what does it matter how much I love anyone when I am not able to take care of them.

What I hate most of all they *all* seemed to think so much of me but by a little explanation they will all be right again.

I saw Ellis Hull yesterday. He seemed oh! so glad to see us. He looks as rough & dirty as the rest of us.

Sister Em you spoke about buying a little negro. Uncle Ezekiel has a might smart little negro (Jinnie). Maybe you could get her. You could write to him & see. Tell him I told you to write. Or perhaps you could buy Nancy from Cos Sam. I will see him or if you think you can learn Polly anything I will write to Mr. A-(?) about it. Maybe Aunt Frank would let you have Mariah. If I was at home I think I could find one.

I saw Jim Turner (?) the day before he left for Geo. He will have a good time I suppose as he will be at home in water melon season. Ask Mother why she does not write to me. I have written to her some two or three times since I received a letter from her. I was just thinking last night that you all had forgotten me. Miss Lou used to write to me oftener than any of you. What did you think of that letter I sent you? Could you see through it? I could. I think I will quit such nonsense. I must stop & get ready for Drill. Tell darkies all howdy. My love to Pa, Mother, *Lizzie, Willie,* Charlie & Kiss Little Bubber often for his Brum. Hoping dear sister to hear from you all soon I am as ever your Loving

   Brum

Tell Mother if I get my commission I will call on her for nice *Sword - (She need not get it yet tell her.)*

(1863--EKA)

July 27 - Aunt Frank after all my hurrying to get my letter of yesterday ready for the mail I was just in time to be too late. So I thought as I had this small piece of paper I would add another word or two. Paper is so very scare or I would write you another letter & try & do better but will send this one this time promising to do better in future. I am really ashamed but hope you will excuse me this time. Tell Miss Eliza I have not heard from her in a long, long time. How is Mittie & Maggie getting on at school. Tell Miss M- I saw Nat a few days ago. He was looking quite well. Henry came in last night from Stanton. Was very glad to see him. Had not seen him since he left me at Williamsport Md. He seems to be enjoying himself very much. The Yankies came very near getting him twice. Aunt Frank I sent to Mother for a coat, & as you are in that *line* I would like you could either make or help make it. I will be under many obligations to you & will pay all damages besides. Please excuse mistakes as it is raining & Dr. Gober & myself are sitting under a blanket & he keeps talking, so I hardly know what I am doing. (*Dr. is now my Capt.*) We have a good time by ourselves. My love to Mr. Kirkham, Misses Eliza, Mittie & Mag. Hoping to hear from you soon I am in haste your

Loving Nephew

W.R. Montgomery

My love to my Sweet Heart if you see her, or if you can find one for me. I am now forsaken. If you know any young lady that wants to marry as soon as I can get home refer them to me, & speak a word in my favor, as I am tired of waiting longer on the war & want some one to *take care of me in my old age.*

Camp 3rd Geo. Batt S.S.
August the 18th 1863

Dear Aunt Frank-

I now drop you these few short lines to inform you that I am quite well & in very good spirits. I wrote to you a few days ago, making two letters in a short time & I am sorry to say I have not heard one word form them yet. Miss Eliza, if I am not mistaken also owes me a letter. Haven't heard form you or any of the family in a long time. Don't know why some of you don't write. I think if I was at home & you out in the Army I would write you (at my leisure any how)

I have no news to communicate to you. We are lying camp waiting for the Yankies, but not like your Army in Tenn, expect to fall back as the enemy advances, but expect to fight & whip them too.

How is Miss E & Mr. Mayer getting on or did he come out at Vicksburg all right.

Hope he did. Heard to day of the death of Mrs. Bowlan Glover, was truly sorry to hear it. Cos Sam, Wm.A & Henry are quite well. Henry came in from Orange Court House yesterday. Have not seen him in some time before. Aunt Frank please hand this letter to Sister Em if she has not gone home & if she is gone send it to her by some reliable person, as it contains a little money. You will please excuse my short note today as I am in great haste. Have to fix up & go on Review in a few minutes. My loves to Misses Eliza, Mittie, Mag & all the family & accept the same of Your Loving Nephew in haste

W.R.Montgomery

Aunt Frank I will write you a letter soon. Hope you will excuse haste. Write soon & tell the rest to write. My love to all friends. My regards to Misses C.C.

On Chickamauga Creek near Ringgold Sept. 20th
1863 (Sunday Evening)

Dear Aunt Frank

We are now lying on the bank of the Chickamauga Creek waiting for rations. Haven't had any since we left Atlanta.

We are in hearing of the fight, prettie heavy cannonading but nothing to compare with Gettysburg. I am very sorry I did not get to stop in Marietta. Expected to see you all. I must stop now as we have orders to move to the Battle field. I will finish when we stop if nothing happens.

Thursday the 24th. Near Chattanooga Tenn. We had a hard fight on Sunday. Took a great many prisoners, also a great many pieces of Artillery. We have driven the Yankies some 10 or 12 miles since Sunday. Are now 1/2 mile from Chattanooga. Had a heavy skirmish day before yesterday evening. Had one man killed in our Co & several wounded.

We are now lying at the foot of Lookout Mt. Had a heavy shelling this morning form the Yankies. Made us get up a little earlier than usual. The Yanks are well fortified here. I saw Gens Bragg, Breckenridge & Polk. Gen Longstreet's corps took a conspicuous part in the fight. Gen Hood was wounded. Also many others.

Aunt Frank I will write again soon if nothing happens. My love to Misses Liza,

Mittie & Mag & all the family. My regards to Miss Lou. Tell her I saw her when I came through M. I am in haste.

Your Loving Nephew

W. R. Montgomery

I have to write on my knee. I have no stamp. Excuse writing. This is a hard country. Worse than Va. Write soon to W.R.H. Co F 3rd Geo Batt S.S.

Camp Lookout near Chattanooga Tenn.
Oct. 16, 1863

My Dear Aunt Frank

'Tis with much pleasure I embrace the opportunity of writing you a few hurried lines to inform you that I am quite well, but I am sorry to inform you that I am not in as good spirits I would like to be, for I assure you I am tired of Gen Bragg & am very anxious to be again in old Va under my favorite Gen (Robert E. Lee) the best man of the age. Aunt Frank I have written to you twice since I passed through Marietta. But I have not heard a word from you or any one else since I left old Va. I have written home I think about half dozen times since I came to this place but not one word do I ever hear in return. I have been looking for a letter from you for two weeks, but it seems you too like the rest have forgotten me. I think I am getting in a prettie fix when Mother, Bro, Sister, Kinfolks & Sweet Heart all forget me or rather discard. I am sure I do not know what all of this is for. Here I've been for nearly one month & only about 100 miles form home only six hours ride, & I have not heard a word from any of you. I really think you treat me meanly. Everybody else can hear from home but myself. I wrote to Mother to send me some potatoes & butter as she lives where they ought to be plentiful but I have looked & looked for them untill I have given up in utter despair. *Why! I was so certain I* would get them I went so far as to ask Col & QrMas to come around and eat with me, but "*no taters*" & what I hate will not be soon I fear.

Capt. Gober left us about a week ago for the hospital, but I expect he is at home before now. It has been raining for three days & the whole face of the earth is about shoe mouth deep in mud & water. I have not been dry since the rain commenced. We have but one tent to the company &

I gave mine up to the sick, so I have no shelter only what I can make of my blanket which I assure you is very poor. Cos Sam & Wm.A- are quite well.

Our Batt has had two heavy engagements since we came to this place. We drove the Yankies back each time. Got out of ammunition each engagement. Had one man killed dead in our Co & several wounded. Gen Bragg's men say that Western Yankies are harder to whip than Eastern Yankies, but is all a mistake. All fight alike. When we give them the Bayonet they give way, they cant stand cold steel. We are encamped near the foot of Lookout Mountain about one & 1/2 miles from & in sight of Chattanooga. Several persons have honored us with a call from Marietta. Mr. Lowrey, Mr. John Barrett & others, but none could tell me anything about you or family. Aunt Frank I really think you ought to write to me. If I was at home & you in the Army I think I would not treat you so badly. Lieut A Ford Johnson said he saw the young ladies often while at home. I was truly sorry the cars did not stop in Marietta as we came through. I had promised myself much pleasure in passing through Marietta from the time we left Va & I really think it too bad we did not stop. I have not got over my "mad" fit about it yet. I would have jumped off anyway but Capt G- was absent & I was in command of the Co. It is rumored in camp that Gen McLaws division is going to Mobile, Ala. Hope it may be so, for any place to get from under Gen Bragg I can, nor do not like him. Don't believe he is competent to fill the place he holds. May be mistaken. Hope I am, but cant believe it.

I heard a few days ago that Miss Lou Boyd is to marry Capt. Williams of Atlanta soon. Write to me soon & tell me all about & all the news in general about Marietta. I hope I may get a furlough when Capt. Gober gets back, if times are quiet.

Aunt Frank tell Walter to Tell Mr. Sanford Dorham to send that haversacks I ordered by first one passing. Hoping you will write soon I will stop. My love to Misses Eliza, Mittie, Maggie & family, and accept of the same for yourself & Mr. K. In haste Your Loving Nephew,
W. R. Montgomery

Excuse haste & all mistakes. Write soon, very soon.

Camp Lookout Mt. near Chattanooga Tenn
Oct. 24th 63

My Dear Aunt Frank
Your kind favor of the 19th inst was most gladly
received day before yesterday. I assure you I was truly
glad to hear from you all. Had not heard from any of you
before since I left *"old" Virginia.* But as your excuse for
not writing is a very good one, I will have to excuse you
for this time. But indeed Aunt Frank I really hope you will
in future do better. I have no news of interest to write you
today. It has been raining for several days, but has now
cleared off & is quite cool. We have no tents yet, so we
have to make out as best we can be stretching our
blankets. So you see when it is cold & raining too we need
our blankets to cover with. I am awful tired of Gen Brag
& this part of the country, & am too anxious to be again
in "old Va" under Gen Lee. But I suppose I ought to be
satisfied. I have not received one letter from home since
here I've been & that was dated the 14th. Henry was to be
up in a few days but no Henry. Aunt Frank I am almost
crazy for something good to eat. Am really afraid those
"old fits will come back on me." - "You remember." One of our
wagoners came in last night & brought me an old hen, so
you ought to have seen me eat chicken & dumplings. You
may be sure they were good, a little tough though. I heard
from Capt Gober the other day, said he would soon be
back & bring us a box. Ellis Hull staid with me last night,
on his way to Quincy, Fla. Has been elected a Lt. in a Regt
at that place. Cos Sam & Bill A. are well. Haven't seem
them though in two or three days.
Well! Miss Lou is married at last. Joy & peace go with
her. Hope she has done well. I feel confident she has done
much better than if she had *"waited"* for me. Miss Lou is
indeed a nice young lady & with but few equals.

The Yankies are all quiet, in front. We now & then have a few shots from our pickets.

When the Chickamauga bridge washed away the other day we had to do without rations for two days. It was hard to be so near home & have to suffer for something to eat. In Va I was used to it. Aunt Frank I do hope you will write often & give me all the news from old Marietta. Tell Miss Eliza I heard about her the other day, have a great deal to tell her when I see her. I do hope you will answer my letter today. I am sitting over an old log fire & the smoke runs me almost crazy. Can't think of anything to write. Saw Mr. Haley today. He was well. My love to Misses Eliza, Mittie, Maggie & family, & write soon to

Your Loving Nephew

W. R. Montgomery

My kindest regards to Mr. K- when you write to him next. I am a thousand times obliged to you for the butter Mr. Lowrey is to bring. Will anxiously await his coming. Write soon to William.

On front line near
Knoxville, Tenn.
Nov. 27th, 1863

My dear Aunt Frank

Your kind letter of the—was most gladly received a few days ago. I assure you I was truly glad to hear from you all. We are now seeing what you might call a hard time & have a little fighting every day. We Sharp Shooters are in front all the time from 100 to 500 yards of the Yankies. We keep up a prettie heavy fire all the time, take a shot whenever a Yankie shows his head. Day before yesterday the 2nd Michigan Regt charged & flanked our rifle pits & drove our Batt back for a while, but we soon rallied, charged and drove them back. The brigade was in the rear, too far to help us, had a prettie hard fight for a while. Our little Batt has only about 130 men for duty. We whipped & drove back one whole Reg of "Yanks" capturing about 60. Our loss was only 2 killed & 3 badly wounded, one from our Co. We killed the Adgt, a fine looking man indeed ..... (illeg.) ..... his sweethearts letters. Killed 2 Lts. the Maj. & about 25 others. Every body tells us it was a gallant affair. I tell you our little Bat fought gallantly. We have ..... (illeg.) ..... wounded & think all will work well for us.

Aunt Frank as regards the butter you sent, I did not hear anything about it, but suppose it was lost, in the Box. I am indeed obliged to you for it anyway. I am surprised that any one should think I acted wrong in any way with Miss Lou. I think I am a free man yet, & have a right to act as I please & not as others. Anyhow I ever will claim that as a right. I once thought a great deal of Miss Lou but I think I had good reasons for not marrying her, reasons that I may tell you some time if live. I would like to know who it is that thinks I am guilty of so grave an *offense.* I think as you do Aunt Frank, some people are always interfering with somebody's business that does not concern them. Please tell me all about it when you next write, also all you have heard from any other source. Aunt Frank I hope you will excuse this badly written letter, as I have no time. Am now on post in the rifle pits, & the Yankies are shooting at us. Have nothing to write on save my knee. I have not heard from home in some time.

A few hours later—Since writing the above Aunt Frank I have just finished the painful task of burying one of our men (was killed). "No useless coffin encloses his breast, but he lays like a brave warrior taking his rest with only his blanket around him." It is awful to think of, to be called upon so suddenly to bury an intimate friend & associate. But such is the fate of War, *cruel War.* Oh! how heartily would we all hail a happy peace. Do write soon Aunt Frank & tell me all the news about old Marietta. I will write you again soon & will try & have more time to do it in. Our Boys keep up a prettie heavy fire all the time. If you could hear us you would think a battle going on. My love to all the family, & write soon to Your Loving Nephew

W. R. Montgomery

Aunt Frank do please excuse my letter today. I am really ashamed to send it now, but paper is so scarce it will not do to back out, "So here goes."

Nov. 29—We had a fight today. Col Ruff & Capt Johnson were both killed.

Camp 3rd Bat Geo S.S.
January 19th 1864

My dear Aunt Frank

'Tis indeed with much pleasure I take my pencil this cold, cold snowy morning to drop you a few hurried lines. We just got in last night from a 3 days march through rain snow & mud & by the way a little hard fighting. I assure you we had a hard time but that is very common now with Longstreets corps. Last Friday night we were aroused & ordered to get up cook rations & be ready to move at daylight. At daylight we took up our march towards Knoxville. Marched about twenty miles through the mud & snow. Had a nice little fight & drove the Yankies back about two miles & then rested such a rest as it was. Had to lay out 3 nights without any covering (in the snow) save the wide expanded arch of Heaven which you may imagine was by no means pleasant. But we arrived again in camp with but little loss on our side which makes us enjoy our little huts the more. Aunt Frank it is enough to make tears come from the eyes of the most hardened soul to see our brave men marching through the mud & snow almost naked & *barefooted*. My feet are on the ground. My shoes are only a little better than none at all. The whole corps is barefooted & in rags. In my company we have but five or six men with shoes. Some of them wear mockersons made of rawhide. I drew four blankets for the Co. the other day & there is yet some four or five men that have not even a single blanket yet. "They say" there is a large supply at Bristol Tenn for us, & will soon be here. I sincerely hope it is true for the men are really suffering.

We are now about 40 miles above Knoxville but we hold the country as far as Strawberry Plains (20 miles of KO). We are now living very well, but I assure you it is quite a late thing. On our march from K—we only had quarter rations of flour no salt or anything else for two or three weeks, & for three days we only drew one ear of corn to the man per day. The campaign in E.T. has indeed been a trying one. Our charge at Knoxville was a most gallant affair if I do tell it myself & you may always know that where Gen Lee's brave and gallant band meets the Yankies they show the true grit of the Southern soldiery. Aunt Frank why don't some of you write to me. Everybody else can get letters from home (Marietta too) but not the first word have I or can I get from home, Marietta or any where else. I have not had a letter in two months from any body. Don't know what to make of it. I suppose the Yankies got some from me, all that was sent to Knoxville or Sweet Water. I heard the other day that Miss Marietta Gramling had married a Capt. Also that the brave and gallant little William had married *but who to*? But write soon and tell me the news about old Marietta the people in general. I suppose *old Pace* (Ardis) has got home. You must be sure and write by him, & if you are too busy tell some of those young ladies to write to their Soldier Cousin. *What do you say*? I must close. My love to Misses Eliza Mittie & Maggie also to Mr. K— & family & write soon to

Your Loving Nephew
W. R. Montgomery

Excuse writing as it is quite cold. The ground is covered in snow & the wind is blowing oh! so cold. I am alone in my little hut in my glory. I have no one since Capt. G left to disturb me of my happy thoughts of Home Sweet Home & by gone days. Oh! the happy days that can never be recalled, but then I was not happy. Why not—simply because I would not, but had I the chance again I think I could. Do tell some of the children to write to their Soldier Cousin & not forget me because I am in the field doing my duty where many others ought to be. I used to think I had friends in Marietta, but I sometimes fear that I was mistaken. *"Out of sight out of mind."* Mighty true. My love to all & write soon, very soon to WRM   In haste

Camp Camden
January 20th 1864

My dear Mother

It is indeed with pleasure that I seat myself to drop
you a few hasty lines although some time has elapsed
since I have heard directly from you. We are all well,
progressing finely. It is now raining very hard & has been
for three or four days & the mud is awful. One half of our
tent is a perfect *mud hole*. The ground has been covered in
snow ever since the night of the 3rd untill day before
yesterday when the rain melted the last. I had the pleasure
of standing six hours on post while it was snowing very
hard & was on picket in it three days, but we got used to
it now & we take it all easy. The last snow we had was in
some places half leg deep & in many places 10 inches. The
weather has indeed been so very bad that we can hardly
get out of our tent without miring up to our knees in
mud. You have no idea what a county this is. I don't
suppose there is a wheel barrow full of sand in the county.
We have orders to move as soon as the weather gets better
about three miles from here on the other side of the run
near the battle ground on the 18th & about 5 miles from
the ground on the 21st. I have nothing of interest to write
you as everything pertaining to camp life is dull.

I have been waiting anxiously indeed a long time for a
letter from some of you. I think *Hen* might give his big *bud*
a few lines anyhow, don't you? We are all now looking
forward to the 8th of April when we will all then be
released for a short while at least. A great many are
reenlisting for the war. I have been thinking of it myself
but have not yet made up my mind fully. Uncle Joe's
Battery is stationed near us, see him nearly every day.,
think of joining his company. I wrote to Bud & Buck a few
days ago. Have not heard from them yet. Saw in the
papers the other day that the 1st Geo was in a fight, had a

hard time of it in the snow. I was & am still uneasy as the Regt lost several. I was over at the 7th Geo a few days since. All the River boys were well as far as I could learn. Scot Brown of the "Wool Hats" died the other day & was sent home by Crawford Tucker. There is a good many deaths now in camp. We lost a might clever little fellow (Paul Miller) in our company only a few days ago.

Times are very hard out here at this time. Had a nice mess of sausage the other morning. Made me think of home. Paid 50 cts per pound for it. Bought a turkey & some eggs last weeks. Like to hurt ourselves. Cooked it by camp fire. Paid $2.50 cts for the turkey & 62 cts for the eggs. Well I must close as it is getting dark. My love to M O & Henry, all friends.

Hoping to hear from you soon. I am your loving son in haste

W. R. Montgomery

Tell Henry if he knows what is good for him he had better write.

(A line cut off sheet. EKA)

Write soon - W R M[1]

---

[1] The letters to Sister Em, Bro, and Bro Chal were given to Mrs. Annie Montgomery DuPre by her brother Geo. F. Montgomery. Sister Em was Emma M. Montgomery (1837-1913) who married Chalmers Poindexter Haynes (1834-1862). They were married in 1855. "Bro" was Joseph S. Montgomery (born 1843, died in Hearne, Texas). Henry, the other brother, was born 1846.

The letters to Aunt Frank were given to Mrs. Jessie Lee Montgomery Anderson by Miss Kate Kilby. Aunt Frank was Margaret Frances Young (1823-1909) who married James T. Kirkham (1812-1878) a widower with several children. They were married 1848. Letters copied by EKA, November 1960.

Marietta Geo. Mar 22nd/66

Miss Emma[2]
"Out of the abundance of the heart the mouth *must* speak." I am alone tonight Miss Emma, thinking of you & the unknown future & whether that future to me, is to be a happy one is for you & you alone to say, for if you be *true* to your promise, yours is the voice that must call me from life's dangerous path & lead me to fix my eyes on the steadily shining light of truth. Your hands are the ones that must strew my pathway through this earthly pilgrimage with brightest flowers. My pathway for the past few years has been a hard & rather unpleasant one & had but few roses to adorn its arduous windings, but Miss Emma if you *truly love me*, I could not ask for *brighter roses*. I had once thought, this cold, selfish & unfriendly world could never afford me the *bliss* for which I had so *often sighed*, but Miss Emma you came like a *Sweet & ministering angel* & found access into the *tenderest* recesses of my soul. Then doubt not that I *love* you. I *love* you *far more* than my own existence. But Miss Emma wealth is not mine to offer you, but if a strong arm and a loving heart & lifelong devotion can make you happy, then know that you are happy already. Oh! Miss Emma if you will *truly love me, tell me, if not tell me* that I may know my fate. My whole heart is yours Miss Emma & I can expect nothing less than yours in return, for I can *not share* your *love* with another.

Miss Emma marriage is rather a grave & a serious subject, a subject that should claim our every thought. We should well understand each other & feel, know that on the one thrives the happiness of the other, for we are to

---

[2] Letter from W. R. Montgomery to his Fiancee, Emma Jane Northcutt.

take the walk of life together. heaven grant that it be a happy one. You are to share with me my cares as well as my joys. You are to be my *sweet* sympathizer in adversity's *dark hour* & your happiness will be my happiness & to know Miss Emma, that when Adversity does come that there will be one true faithful & loving heart to sympathize with me & one bright & cheerful smile to cheer me in my gloom, will be a happiness that I had long since ceased to hope for in this *life*.

"Oh! woman, woman, truly thou art God's noblest creation, What would this world be without thee."

Man perplexed & annoyed by the cares & toils of the busy world goes home at night & is soon soothed to rest by the music of the kindly coined words of a Loving *Wife*. What greater boon could man ask, but how many oh! yes how many are rendered miserable for life by unhappy marriage. Heaven forbid that such a *union be ours*.

I am sad & lonely tonight Miss Emma & pleasant thoughts are but a mockery. Oh! how often, how often have I wished that time ... (torn and part of letter lost. EKA) ..... wing & hasten on with accel ... long, long wish ... & not until then ... visiting you this ... of the weather. I was denied that pleasure, but I hope to see you very soon.

Tis late, late Miss Emma & the mournful sounds of the whistling winds summon me to my couch to dream, ah! yes to *dream sweet dreams of thee. May Guardian angels* ever watch over & SHIELD YOU FROM *ALL* HARM is the wish of one who *devotedly loves you*.

Resptfly yours,

W. R. Mont--------

Please forgive this intrusion for I am suffering with the "Blues" as I was disappointed in not seeing you this evening, but hope to see you as soon as my return from the river.

W.R.M.

To Miss Emma[3]
"I would not kiss the sweetest lip
Unless it kissed me too;
As well from the young rose-bud sip,
The morning's clear cold dew.

Nor clasp a hand, though soft & warm,
Unless it pressed mine own;
I' rather love the perfect form
Carved out of Parisian stone.

I will not worship eyes though bright
And beautiful they be,
Unless they bend their loving light
On me - *and only me*!

I would not love a form that heaven
Its self hath stamped divine,
If I but dreamed its love was given
To other hearts than mine."
                              Respcfly Yours &c
                              W. R. Mont------
Marietta Geo.
May 1st 1866

---

[3] The following was written in the Autograph Album of Emma Jane
Northcutt. The Autograph Album and the letter from W.R.M. to Emma
Northcutt were among papers given by W.R.M. to his daughter Mrs.
Jessie Lee Montgomery Anderson. He gave her, also, the Commission
and the Furlough Paper. (Copied by EKA November 1960).

Letter from A. W. Whitehead, 200 Academy St., Newark, N. J., Mar. 27, 1907:

Capt. W. R. Montgomery
Marietta, Ga.

My Dear Sir:
Last May I met you and your Son, Geo. F., in the Exchange Hotel at Fredricksburg, Va.

You informed me that you had a sword[4] taken from a dying Union soldier (Major) on the battlefield of Gettysburg, Pa. which you would like to return to his family, or friends if they could be traced up.

I have investigated the matter thoroughly since I came home and the following is the result. His name was Louis Francine, and at the time you met him he was Colonel of the 7th N. J. V. Infty, having been commissioned only a day or two before, but had not changed his straps as Major. He did not die on the field as you expected but was taken to a Hospital & died July 1st, 1863. Now a little on his earlier career. When the Civil War began, he was Captain of a fire company, Philadelphia, Pa., and raised Co. A of the 7th Jersey from the firemen. Of course he was then made Captain, and for bravery on the field of battle, was made a Major, & next a Col.

As near as I can trace him in Philadelphia, his people are all dead.

Some of the old firemen, who remember him, say that he lived with is mother & a sister, who have long since crossed the *River*. So, of course, it will be impossible to return the sword to any of his relatives; but I would like to

---

[4] The Correspondence about the Sword of W.R.M. and the Sword itself were given to Mrs. Annie Montgomery DuPre by her brother Geo. F. Montgomery.

have it returned to Lincoln Post No. 11 G.A.R. Dept. of N.J. if you so desire.

Quite a number of his regiment are members of said Post, and I have no doubt but what the gift would be highly appreciated by them.

If you think well enough of this proposition, it can be shipped to my address, at my expense, and I will turn it over to the Post, using your name &c.

Or, I can place you in communication with the Post Commander, and you can negotiate that way.

However, let me hear from you whether for or against it, when convenient.

Enclosed stamped envelope for reply.

Respectfully Yrs

A. W. Whitehead

P.S. Are you off or from?

Letter from A. W. WHITEHEAD, April 29, 1907, to G. F. Montgomery, Esq.[5]

"Your decision in regard to Sword is all right. I thank you sincerely for the attention you haven given the subject. We have a flag taken form the 14th Ga. Infty at Spottsylvania C.H. Va. which we prize very highly, and would not like to part with either on the same ground that you mention. Merely an heirloom."

---

[5] This letter is yet another from A. W. Whitehead thanking WRM for a letter just read and regretting to hear of "your father's death. the Vets of both sides are fast passing away. When we are *all* gone *surely* the Civil War will be over." Mentions Reunion plans and experiences.

Letter to George F. Montgomery, Esq. from T. F. Swayze, Office of the Secretary Treasury Department, Washington D.C., June 13, 1907:

...*"sorry to learn, from Comrade Whitehead, of your father's death, for I greatly enjoyed my short acquaintance with him and yourself last year on the occasion of our pilgrimage to the battle fields of Fredricksburg and vicinity.

... Reunion plans ...

"These meetings with the brave men of the Confederate army and talking over our battle of 1861 to 1865 gives me a pleasure that I cannot describe. Therefore I can readily understand how much your father must have enjoyed meeting us at Fredricksburg; and it will give you a life-long pleasure to remember that you were able to give him this great pleasure just before he left you to join the loved ones gone before.

Now, with reference to the sword which your father so magnanimously offered to restore to any member of the family of the soldier who lost it, I wish to say, as president of our regimental association at the time this generous offer was made, that you are entitled to keep the sword, and ought to keep it as an evidence of your father's bravery and loyalty to a cause that he believed to be right and righteous."

Copy of reply to Mr. Swayze by Geo. F. Montgomery, Secretary, Office of the Railroad Commission of Georgia, State Capitol, Atlanta, July 22, 1908. (Mr. Swayze's letter had been misplaced therefore delay in answering.)

I note that your regimental association shortly before you wrote me had another pilgrimage, that time to Gettysburg, etc., and that you had a nice time, being received cordially by your former enemies. I know that these trips must be the source of great pleasure to all of you, as the one my father and I took was to us. You can never know how much we enjoyed our trip, and especially meeting you and your friends, and spending the evening together as we did. I doubt that a better soldier ever went to the front then my father. He was in every battle of consequence fought by the Army of Virginia and in addition came all the way to Georgia with Longstreet and was in the engagements at Chicamauga and Knoxville. I have often thought that had every soldier in both armies been like him, excepting of course the action or control of Providence, the war would either have ended quicker or been going on yet. He was never re-constructed but always had the kindliest feelings for those on the other side, especially if they were, as I know you and your friends were, good soldiers. One of the richest heritages from my father is his record as a soldier, and the assurance I have that he did well his part, and saw service almost unequalled.

Yes, as you say, death never comes at the right time, or rather we always fight and grieve at its coming, but my father was tired, and often said the he would like to go. He had no disease whatever except a broken-heart because of his absent wife. His strength slowly wasted and several days before the end his memory failed, and when he was not asking for or talking about mother, it was the war. I trust that you will pardon so much personality, but your kind letter struck a responsive chord in my heart, and the echo can still be heard. But I hope one of these days we will all join hands together in that land that knows no war, and where there will be no more going out.

As you suggest, I want to keep my father's sword—it is testimony as to his service.

AFTERWORD

William Rhadamanthus Montgomery moved to Dekalb County in 1850 not long after his father's death. He was one of the most honored and respected citizens of Marietta, Georgia. Not only was he an officer during the war, he was for many years elected to public office and managed his own dry goods and grocery business.

In 1866 he was married to Emma Jane Northcutt, a member of another prominent Marietta family. They had six children: Jessie (24 June 1867–5 February 1945); George (); Mamie E. (14 March 1874–6 September 1920); Julia Pearl (6 July 1877–31 July 1879); Nellie May (8 November 1880–13 August 1881); Willie (10 September 1882–2 September 1886). With three children dying before their fourth birthdays, the Montgomery's lived a saddened life. In 1868 they moved to Hickory Flat in Cherokee County, returning to Marietta in 1874.

But WRM continued to be in the public eye. Available documents reveal that he was both the Clerk of the Superior Court and County Treasurer simultaneously on at least two occasions.[1] His involvement in politics and law were more substantial than this, however, as he was a very influential individual in the community. He was elected as County Clerk a total of ten times, serving for twenty years.

On 21 July 1894, his wife Emma died. Shortly thereafter, he married Anna Towers, daughter of Colonel John Towers of Marietta. William Rhadamanthus Montgomery died 30 November 1906.

---

[1] On 8 January 1883 and 14 October 1896. He was Countyr Treasuerer also by the date of 11 January 1881.

APPENDIX

Commission of W. R. Montgomery

Confederate States of America
War Department
Richmond
June 17th 1863

Sir:
You are hereby informed that the President has appointed you
First Lieutenant,
3rd Georgia Battalion, Sharp Shooters

In the Provisional Army in the service of the Confederate States: to rank as such from the Ninth day of June one thousand eight hundred and sixty three. Should the Senate, at their next session, advise and consent thereto, you will be commissioned accordingly.

Immediately on receipt hereof, please to communicate to this Department through the Adjutant and Inspector General's Office, your acceptance or non—acceptance of said appointment; and with your letter of acceptance, return to the Adjutant and Inspector General the OATH, herewith enclosed, properly filled up, SUBSCRIBED and ATTESTED, reporting at the same time your AGE, RESIDENCE, when appointed, and the STATE in which you were BORN.

Should you accept, you will report for duty to Lt. Col. Hutchins.

James A. Seddon
Secretary of War
Lieut W. R. Montgomery

3rd Geo: Battalion
Sharp Shooters

Furlough paper of W. R. Montgomery

3 Batt Geo S S
January 17th 1865
Col W. H. Taylor
    A. A. Genl
    I respectfully ask leave of absence for thirty (30) days to visit my home near Atlanta Geo. My family have been driven from their home by the enemy who burned and destroyed house and furniture & robbed them of everything in the way of subsistence. I therefore ask this indulgence that I may if possible do something for their comfort. I am almost entirely destitute of comfortable clothing, & it is impossible to procure them here in the Army. The company is small 26 men for duty. Capt. & 2nd Lt. are both present. I received a leave of indulgence about 12 months ago while in East Tenn.
    I am Col with much respect
    Your obd sevt
    W. R. Montgomery 1st Lt
    Co F 3d Batt Geo S S

(Written on back of application)
Co F 3d Geo S S
17th January 1865

— —

Lt. W. R. Montgomery

— —

Thirty (30) days

— —

Application for leave of absence
Respectly forwarded
Approved
    N. N. Gober
    Capt. Co F 3d Batt

— —

HdQrs 3d Geo Batt
17 Jany 1865
Respectfully forwarded approved —
though one of the officers
(the 2d Lieut) present is not
for duty
    N L Hutchins Jr
    Lt. Col Comdg
     — —

Brig Hd Qrs Jan 17th 65
Respy fow'd approved
    D. M. DuBose
    Brig Gen'l

Hdqrs Kershaw Div
    Jan 19 65
Res — forwarded approved
    J.B.Kershaw
    Maj Genl
     — —

HdQrs 1 Army Corp
    Jny 21, 1865
Res retd for compliance
with G.O. No 4 from these
Hdqrs by Command of
G G LtGen Longstreet
Feb 6   O. Latrobe
Jan 21   Adj (?)
     — —

HdQrs Battery
    24 Jany 65
There are for duty
Field Staff (including a Cadet) 3
Co. Officers   7
      Total   10
Officers: None absent on leave,
One applying under this application
…......(Illeg.)

Duty — total present   86 men
  N. L. Hutchins Jr. Lt.Col.Comdg
       — —

Brig HdQrs Jan 26 '65
Respy for'd appd
    D.M.DuBose Brig Gen
       — —

HdQrs Kershaw Div
    Jan 28 65
Res — forwarded approved
    J.B.Kershaw   Maj Genl

HdQurs 1st A Corps
    Jan 31 65
Res ford appd for 24 days
For Lt Genl Longstreet
    O Latrobe
    A A Genl
       — —

Approved for twenty
four (24) days
By order of Gen. Lee
    W. H. Taylor
Feb 16 '65   A.A.G
1856 M
       — —

App Chf   C.S.
Rich'd Feby 6th 65
Five days subst. issd
    F.T.Forbes
    Capt. & Ch.F.C.S.
       — —

Furlough to take effect
from the 27th February 1865
    J.W.Williams   Adjt
       — —

(Stamped on face of application)

Transportation Furnished in Kind Home—
Richmond Va. L.H.Wood Major & W.M.

(Written beside stamp) & Back to Augusta Ga.

— —

(Attached paper)   HdQrs 3 Bat Geo
S.S.

Feb. 24th 1865

I certify that Lt. W. R. Montgomery entered the
service as a Private & that he served for more than
two years in that capacity. He has never recd
transportation home & aback while on furlough of
indulgence under act of Congress.

N. N.Gober Capt
Comdg 3d Batt Geo S.S.

Index